WRITING FOR LOVE

P9-DUV-755

991

DATE DUE

~~JY 30 '92~~			
JY 11 '96			
MR 5 '97			

WRITING
FOR LOVE
AND MONEY

OTHER BOOKS BY KATHRIN PERUTZ

NOVELS

Reigning Passions
Mother Is a Country
The Ghosts
A House on the Sound
The Garden

NONFICTION

Marriage is Hell
Beyond the Looking Glass: America's Beauty Culture

WRITING
FOR LOVE
AND MONEY

KATHRIN PERUTZ

THE UNIVERSITY OF ARKANSAS PRESS

FAYETTEVILLE   1991

This book was designed by Chiquita Babb using the typeface Galliard.

The paper used in this publication meets the minimum requirements of
the American National Standard for Permanence of Paper for Printed
Library Materials z39.48-1984. ∞

Library of Congress Cataloging-in-Publication Data

Perutz, Kathrin, 1939–
    Writing for love and money / Kathrin Perutz.
        p. cm.
        ISBN 1-55728-211-0 (alk. paper). — ISBN 1-55728-212-9 (pbk. :
    alk. paper)
        I. Title.
    PS3566.E73W75   1991
    813'.54—dc20   91-16721
                                                                CIP

Acknowledgments

Initial thanks to the V.C.C.A. for the time and place; to J. McK. of U.K.M.C. for giving me the title one year, an audience another; to M.W. for leaving the lights on; and finally, to J. T. for helping me take out the garbage. Thanks also to the characters, real or otherwise, who made this book possible.

For Becky and Pritchard,

whoever they may be

Contents

I: Love and Money   1

II: Vines   23

III: The Truth in Fiction   47

IV: What Is a Commercial Novel?   69

V: Production   97

VI: The Frog and I   113

WRITING
FOR LOVE
AND MONEY

I

LOVE AND MONEY

He was a small round man balding on top and expanding at the middle. "You'll make me rich," he repeated.

"As the pimp said to the whore."

"Right." He smiled. "Why not?"

We walked across Seventh Avenue, headed for Greenwich. It was a crisp autumn day, late October, the air clear and starched after early morning rain, and on the streets of the Village people were moving with the invigorated gait of midtown, as though they'd all just signed a fat contract and were hurrying toward the nearest tax shelter. I felt a mixture of elation and depression, that commingling of emotions diagnosed as synesthesia in the eighteenth century and serenaded as spring fever in the twentieth. But it was Fall now, I was getting older, I hadn't had a novel published in many years, and I was walking across Seventh Avenue preparing to make a Faustian compact with a little man whose nose and spectacles resembled the masks being sold at Woolworth's for Halloween and whose eyes were Muddy Waters, the name of a singer on a poster we passed. My sense of elation was as friable as the joy that comes with buying a lottery ticket, when you feel, even as you put down your money, that the magic numbers have already assembled to win you the jackpot, though an underlying *Weltschmerz* tells you you don't have a chance in Hell.

"Rich," he said again, exhaling the word like a long-deprived smoker reunited with his weed. "We'll ask three hundred thousand for the second book, a million for the third."

"What if I can't write this one?"

"Don't worry," he said. "You'll write it."

Reasonably, I knew the chances were slim to nonexistent. If I were capable of writing a best-seller, I would have done it long ago. I was not the sort of person who wins the lottery, gets free trips around the world, had an affair with Marlon Brando (in the sixties), or writes books that become best-sellers. It was more than twenty years since my first novel had been published, and though I'd written several books since then, my earnings had never exceeded my expenses by much more than the cost of a few burgers. I was what was known as a "literary" writer (later, "midlist"), meaning that my books were reviewed in the *New York Times Book Review*, and that I received acknowledgment from my peers without being in any danger of falling into the moral turpitude that comes with actually making money from what you write. The five-hundred-dollar advance I received for my first novel was never made up, notwithstanding the photograph on the back jacket showing the Author as Sexpot-about-to-boil-over. The reviews were fine, though, and convinced me, at twenty-one, that I indeed had the Calling. I'd been summoned, and not as a novitiate either, but as someone preordained, a candidate for beatitude who'd been granted a free pass into the empyrean where Shakespeare, Dostoyevsky and the rest of us immortals ruled—the kind of nonsense that comes from being an atheist too young and therefore believing in the redemptive power of words.

Set in that fair field of Enna where Milton gathered laurels, I labored under the delusion—no less ecstatic for being unfounded—that I stood in direct line of succession. It didn't matter that I wasn't a poet, that comparisons with Milton and Shakespeare might be inappropriate to the writer of a small book of fiction; poet and novelist were but different manifestations of the concept of Author. Perhaps it was my early exposure to the German language (my parents were born in the Austro-Hungarian empire) that contributed to my later obfuscation, since the German word "Dichter," which means "poet," is applied also to novelists above a certain rank. Thomas Mann (who wrote *Doctor Faustus*) is a Dichter sure, though so is Goethe, who actually was. In Austria, it is a mark of respect to confer a title upon someone who has no claim to it. My father, a businessman, was usually addressed as Herr Doktor or Herr Professor on our trips abroad; a former colleague of his, heir to a brewery, was ceremoniously deferred to as Herr Baron.

Whether it was from this tradition of linguistic hand-me-downs, or from the more direct influence of leftover nineteenth-century Romanticism still being served out in literary anthologies for college students in the late fifties, I contracted a hyperbolic sense of my existence as a writer. Becoming a writer gave me more than identity, much more than a job. It was my metamorphosis, catapulting me from the cocoon of the ordinary; it gave me wings.

When William Saroyan was asked why he'd wanted to become a writer, he replied, "So I could screw starlets." I understood what he meant. Becoming a writer was to become desirable. Beautiful.

Deathless. God and starlet were heads and tails of the same coin. God is love, after all, the putter-in and taker-out, the giver and receiver. Today's evangelists have brought the synonymity of God and sex into the family living room, where perhaps it belonged all along, but to those of us in the fall-out generation, brought to first tumescence by Elvis the Pelvis, it was still something of a revelation. And because, in those halcyon days of blue balls and quaint virginity, a woman was object (and subject) of desire, but never its author, being both a woman and a writer meant I was Saroyan and starlet in one.

But that was in another era. Literature did not then refer to handouts by software manufacturers and sex was not a fact but an intention. Men were like ships at sea, sailing uncharted waters toward a known destination. Women were like the locks of the Panama Canal, sealing all entry until the password was spoken—"I do!"—and then the floodgates opened and the ship sailed home. (Attempts to block the metaphor were overridden.) In those days I set my course for England and shifted sexes once I got there. I wasn't aware of it at the time and no anatomical disturbances took place. On the contrary, I became more a woman for it. A broad, in the sixties: I shifted my allegiance without realizing that I did, changing horses in midstream, values in mid-ocean, choosing male over female. In the days when sex was baseball, it was acceptable (and even admirable) for prenuptial American males to try balling whatever they could, any chance they could get, just so long as they didn't marry it—a variation on the Marxist credo (Groucho's) that you wouldn't want to belong to a club that would have you.

For unmarried females it was far worse. Encouraged to lead on all comers, they were also expected to hold the line at chastity, that virtuous tissue to be later rendered as an earnest against a ring of gold. The results were dreadful, of course: half yes and half no, unsatisfied and unsatisfying, the demi-vierges turned on their prey like cat and mouse, winning the game but losing the candle.

Between male and female, the choice was obvious, and on the broad back of the Atlantic I loosened my ties with home (which was not to be secured this side of matrimony) and sought harbor in England, cradle of our literature where Lady Macbeth implored the night, "Unsex me here."

Free and twenty-one, washed up on the shores of civility and promiscuity, I rented a flat in North London, at the Archway, with a red satin cover on my bed and a mirrored ceiling above it. In the other room, a parade of china totems lined the mantelpiece: puppy dogs and bunnies, madonnas and pussy cats. I stashed these away along with the birded-and-flowered scatter rugs and placed my boxy Underwood on the pop-up vinyl table anchored to the wall. I began to write.

My second novel (the back cover presenting the Author as Sophisticate in plunging back, corolla'd by cigarette smoke, wine glass in hand) was chosen as Fiction of the Week by the *Observer,* and reviewed in the *New Statesman* as a "minor masterpiece." The third was a mistake, though a published one, and my fourth, a satirical novel written when I was back in America again, placed me in the Top Ten of *Newsweek*'s list of Young Writers to Watch.

All of this had happened before I was twenty-six, or before I married, the two events coinciding in the same year. After that, everything slowed down. I still wrote, but I'd begun to doubt myself, and my publications were becoming more infrequent. I wrote a couple of nonfiction books, a historical novel; I tried my hand at porn, hack jobs, ghost for hire, and did occasional journalism. My latest book—the novel—had been published nearly four years earlier, had come and gone without a single notice to mark its passing as it slid off the flat end of the earth unreviewed, unread, unadvertised. Since then I'd done nothing but write proposals for what I might write if I could, casting my baited hooks in hopes of an editor's nibble. Once in a while I got one, and was assigned to write the piece, but even then my catch usually got away in the end, and I was sinking into the unrewarding and unrewarded sump of middle age doing no more than collecting kill fees for articles first commissioned and later scrapped. I was becoming pusillanimous and paranoid, filled with self-doubt and unwilling to try something new in fear that it would prove unacceptable. I drank a lot, even by my own standards, and quarreled steadily with my husband. Sometimes I would even try to imitate my former self, style and themes, caught in a Wordsworthian time warp wherein the child is mother to the woman. The bright future of my twenties had been extinguished; I'd gone straight from "promising" to has-been with nothing in between. "A has-been who never-was," I joked darkly in the cups of my timorous grief.

When the call came, I said sure. A commercial novel? Nothing to it—though I had no idea what this could be: something like an industrial vacuum cleaner compared to the household model? I'd be working with a collaborator, I learned; the novel was set against a background of wine (the heroine was a queen of the vineyards, a kind of female Baron Rothschild), and I'd be right at home with the subject because of the book I'd written about food.

Not exactly. That book, published in the seventies, had been on the feeding habits of Americans, reflecting the changing tastes of upward mobility. It had little to say about the foods themselves, and less about beverages. Mainly, it was a psycho-sociological examination of who eats what and when, how eating habits fluctuate with income and expectations, the subtleties of eating "up," and other niceties of conspicuous consumption. *The Gorge Rises* was what my friend V had suggested I call it, though it was actually published under the quasi-academic, self-consciously humorous title given it by my editor: *The Care and Feeding of America*. That book, for which I'd received my largest life advance ($10,000), all of which was swallowed up in two years of research and travel, contained absolutely nothing about wines. Nevertheless, through the mysterious transubstantiations possible in the world of publishing, it now qualified me as something of an expert on them.

I phoned the collaborator, Richard Gernreich ("gern reich": the name was serendipity, I felt—it boded wealth) and agreed to meet him at the Riviera on Sheridan Square at eleven the next morning. He'd be sitting near the door, he said, wearing a green turtleneck.

He was dispatching an apple pie à la mode when I arrived, hastily tucking its remains into the pockets of his cheeks before he looked up and greeted me. I took the seat opposite, refused his offer of pie, and settled instead for an unassuming, perhaps overly inconspicuous cup of black coffee. He asked me to tell him something about myself and seemed satisfied when I did, though he was less interested in the books I'd written than in the fact that I could speak French and that my father had kept a wine cellar at home when I was growing up. He wanted to know what my father did and what my husband did and also if I had children. He ordered a cappuccino and after that asked the waitress to bring him a hamburger deluxe. It was lunchtime now, he explained.

Reaching underneath his chair he brought out a hefty parcel wrapped in brown paper and placed it on the table, patting it gently. The outline. "It's fabulous," he confessed. "It's got everything in it. Glamor, hardship—it goes back to the days of the Bible and ends in Hollywood. It's the story of a woman's quest, of a dream she pursues despite all obstacles. The dream . . ." He paused, holding the suspense with the tines of his fork pitched heavenward—
" . . . of Champagne! To produce the finest champagne ever made."

He laid down the fork and leaned across the table. "Think of it! Think nectar, think ambrosia. Wine of the gods, the romance of the grape that's been going on since the time of Noah. Since earlier than that, even. 'Keepers of the vine'—it's the second oldest profession. Bet you didn't know that. It's a proven fact, though, men have been tending vineyards since the very beginning, way back in Egypt, back in the Stone Age. The people at Harrier were crazy for it when I told them, they're planning to use it in promoting the book."

"The Second Oldest Profession?"

"That's right, and the great part about it is that the vineyard keeper's a woman."

"Is that the title? The Second . . . "

"Of course not. You'd never sell on a title like that, not these days. You want a title that's simple and straightforward, easy to remember, but with an aura too. Like *Roots*. You want something classy, something that appeals to women readers, vines."

"I beg your pardon?"

"*Vines*. It's called *Vines*—same kind of thing as *Roots* but it has a more feminine ring."

As in clinging? I wondered. I asked him for the name of the author.

"It's classy too. Jacqueline Knightsbridge. The name alone could be worth thousands, even without the book, but the book's fabulous, you'll see." He patted the parcel again.

"How long is the outline?"

"Two hundred and three pages, exactly."

I sipped my coffee as though what he'd said was nothing unusual. But I was calculating furiously: the outline for *Care and Feeding* had been ten pages, exactly. The finished typescript had come to nearly 500 pages (385 pages in print). Figuring on a rough scale of 1:50, this meant that *Vines* would run close to 10,000 typed pages, or roughly 2,800,000 words.

"Is that a customary length for a book—an outline, I mean, of this kind?" I asked in a nonchalant tone of voice, the way you might ask a cannibal if it was customary to start with the toes.

"It's a bit long," he admitted. "But only because this is the first. After this one, Knightsbridge will be up there with the stars, Judith Krantz, Jackie Collins . . . " He ran his tongue between his lips, savoring future success. "*Vines* will establish her track record, and after that the publishers won't care much what's in the book, just so long as she's the author."

"I can't wait to read the outline," I told him, keeping my face perfectly straight.

He tucked it under his arm and we stepped out into the October sunshine. As we crossed Seventh Avenue he told me I would make him rich. I had serious doubts, but the air was so clear, people were moving with such urgency that for a moment the proposition seemed almost within reach, tangible as the gold ring of a merry-go-round which, if you caught it, would let you have a second ride, another chance free.

When we came up to my car, an aging (though nonvintage) Chevy, he gave a few playful kicks to the front tires and handed me the parcel. "When you've written this," he said, "you can go out and buy yourself a Porsche."

"I'm not sure . . . " I said judiciously.

"A BMW, Ferrari, Alfa-Romeo."

"We'll see." I was feeling nervous again.

"Don't worry, you can do it. I've got a gut feeling about this. You're my girl." The way he was smiling made me almost believe him—like the Master of Ceremonies in a Miss America pageant who's already peeked at the name of the winner. "A Rolls," he went on. "Get yourself a Rolls with a driver."

"I don't think so." But it was too late, I was infected. "I could have the kitchen fixed. New windows, a restaurant-type stove, have the whole thing redone . . . "

"Get a house! Build yourself a house in Florida!"

"Or France . . . "

"Yes!" He was exhilarated, already at work on the outline of my new life. "France is much better, and you can take it all off taxes."

"France?"

"Expenses! Research!"

He was telegraphic in his enthusiasm, but I understood: "That's right, champagne."

"She makes it in California, of course, but a section of the book is set in France."

Foreboding sat on my tongue like cat's fur. I stopped smiling. "She makes champagne in California?"

"That's right. The finest in the world."

"But she can't! I mean, it's not champagne. The word refers only to wines made in the province of Champagne. In France."

"It doesn't matter."

"No, I mean, yes, it does. *Appellation contrôlée*. It's regulated."

"Nobody'll notice."

"But it's like cognac," I appealed. "Cognac can't be cognac unless it comes from Cognac." The syllables clicked like castanets, making a buzz of meaning. "Otherwise"—I clicked them off—"it's brandy."

"Doesn't matter," he repeated. "This is a novel, not a guide to fine wines. A novel is fantasy, invention—you don't have to stick to facts."

"But . . . " I stopped. I nodded, realizing that only a moment ago I had been squandering the Knightsbridge fortune, seeing myself already as the rich and successful—not less for being pseudonymous—author I would become. Why not? Why argue? If Champagne had to be moved to California, or possibly be wiped off the map altogether, it was no concern of mine. My name wouldn't be on the book; who would know? I could hush up the matter of *appellation contrôlée* and no one would be the wiser. I got into the car, placed the outline on the seat next to me and promised Gernreich I'd have it read by the following morning.

"Call me when you're finished," he said. "I know you'll love it."

A terrible sensation of choking came over me. The words *I Want to Throw Up* flashed before my eyes. It was probably the worst thing I'd ever read.

I phoned my friend V, who had read more books than anyone I knew and had also written several. "I can't possibly do this," I said.

"Why not?"

Melodrama compounded by inaccuracies, characters with no more life to them than cutout silhouettes indicating the Ladies room, clichés tumbling like avalanches . . .

"Raining cats and dogs," V corrected.

"I can't do it," I repeated. "It stinks."

"So what?"

"So what *what?* It's garbage, crap, it doesn't even make sense, it's tasteless, vulgar . . . " and so on, until the *obiter dictum:* "it's *immoral.*"

"You could make a lot of money."

"Money?" V the elitist, upholder of standards, going to seed before my very ears? Mammon's apologist? an acolyte of trash? "What's come over you?" I asked, with a solicitude usually reserved for the terminally ill or only marginally sane.

"Money is necessary."

"I'm telling you it's the Devil's work, V."

"Money is held in the highest regard by the people who are most highly regarded."

"I must have the wrong number. I'll call back later."

"Wait a minute. Is it possible you never digested the meaning of that book you wrote, what was it called?"

"The Gorge Rises?"

"That's right. You argue that people like to show they're better than others by the way they eat. The person who has dinner at eight is smarter than folks who dine at six. In our culture, eating rabbit food shows you're a lot more powerful than somebody who chews the fat of hogs. Am I right? Of course I am. Did it never occur to you then, in all your ruminations and mastications on the theme, that the ample flesh adorning the buttocks of women in proverbial fattening houses is no different from the fat rocks sitting on the gaunt fingers of our Western lovelies?—except for their density of course and molecular deviations."

"Talk straight."

"I'm saying that yams in famine, cattle to the Masai and the goats of Greek peasant hospitality all exist on the same moral stratum as our own inestimable money. There's nothing you can do to change it—money is a confirmation of our worth."

"You should be a writer," I said, meanly.

"Never mind. I forgive you."

"So you really think I should go through with it? Write the drivel?"

"You'll never know until you try."

The expert speaking: as far as I knew, there was nothing, or at least nothing commonly available to our species, that V hadn't tried. The books, the paintings, the lovers, the costumes. Changing weight and shape, a veritable Proteus, who could masquerade in her own skin as both male and female. We'd known each other a long time, since before I married; we'd met in a bar in New York in the space between London and wedlock.

She was called Harry when we were first introduced and later she was Venus (during a brief stint as a showgirl), and after that she called herself Dr. Raven, though her family name was Fox. She'd been born male (or at least taken for one), but had become so radiant in her revealed or acquired sex that I decided to call her Vixen. She liked the name, for its sound mainly, but, because it reminded her of her actual sir-name and also because it conjured up certain vulpine habits she took exception to, she asked that I lop off the tail of the word and content myself with its initial letter —an excellent one, she assured me, since it bore iconographic resemblance to the raised arms of welcome, the sign for victory or "up yours," and the delta of Venus, while simultaneously being the alphabetic gate into such words as vetch, verse and vice (and of course, vice versa), all of which she admired. The name stuck, and so did our friendship, which took on a protean character of its own over the years. We were well-matched, complementary, though not yin and yang so much as the weighted ends of a seesaw, teeter-tottering in our roles toward each other, confidants and companions and also the other thing, though not much of that anymore. It had been an interlude, or prelude, rather, at the beginning. She—sometimes it was he—remained the person I could count on, either to bring me down to earth or raise me to the skies, the one who knew me inside out, with whom I'd never been other than myself.

"But if I do this . . . won't it affect my writing?"

"About time. For the past years you've been writing like a two-toed sloth."

"That's not a kind thing to say."

"Maybe not. But anything would be better than those godawful etiolated academics you had in your last book, rambling on about Cartesian philosophy and Wittgenstein instead of getting on with their dinner and getting it off in bed."

"You'd rather I dangle them from the edge of a cliff one thousand feet above the ground, fingernails grasping at the precipice as they debate the *Tractatus*?"

"You see? You're a natural."

"Suppose I throw up?"

V's first novel, a *Bildungsroman*, had originally been titled *Throwing Up*, before the publishers substituted a "G" for the initial cluster. "Go ahead," she said. "And then write the book."

"You really think I can?"

"A purist like you? Of course not. It would turn you into a vegetarian. A vulgarian. Your husband will leave you and your friends will disown you. You'll be filthy rich and surrounded by sycophants."

"O.K.," I said. "You win."

"Fine. Call Malady in the morning and tell her you'll do it."

The Agent: Malady

Melody Krassner was known as Malady to those of her clients who felt she'd placed us in quarantine. (The successful ones probably called her Harmony, for all I knew.) Malady and I had been together for fourteen years, not including the last one.

It was a measure of my relationship with my agent that when she'd called about the commercial novel, it had been more than a year since I'd fired her. She'd never noticed, of course. How could she? An agent of her status was above answering phone calls or replying to letters from clients like myself, the multitudes of would-be or once-were writers from whose expected annual income she couldn't hope to extract a percentage fee that would cover even the most frugal meal at La Cocotte, where she regularly took her successful authors to lunch.

A commercial novel about wines, she said, which were up my alley. "Sure," I said, and "Why not?" though actually I was close to speechless. (In the unlikely event that someone reading this is not himself or herself a writer, let me explain: a call from your agent is like a call from God. When I picked up the phone and heard Malady at the other end, I felt like Lyndon Johnson, roused in the night by the voice of his Supreme Commander issuing directives for the next day's maneuvers in Vietnam. It was a bolt from the blue, a voice coming from left field in the sixth game of the 1986 World Series to tell Mookie where the ball should go.)

I hardly recognized her in the first moment, it had been so long. Like other important agents, Malady considered it extraneous to identify herself when she called. Agents know that their writers sit by the phone all day, staring and glowering at it, praying to it, feeding it whatever witchcraft they're capable of to make it deliver up their agent's voice. The President of the United States doesn't have to identify himself and neither does the Pope or the Higher Deity. When God speaks to a simple farmgirl for instance, he will call her by name (Joan or, if he's speaking French, Jeanne), but will never say, This here's God calling, or: You'll never guess who this is, or: Hello there, this is a voice from your past, or even: Hi, Joan, this is Dad (*"Allô Jeannette, ici parle ton Papa"*).

Neither will an agent say who's calling. Instead, there'll be a peremptory order—"Take down this number," or "There's some-one at Doubleday you should get in touch with," or even "Drop everything"—a command so startling and rare that it inevitably results in the receiver clattering to the floor, a scrambled search to retrieve it, and then only the lonely wait of a dial tone to let you know that the agent has already explained whatever it is you're to drop everything for and is now occupied in ignoring her other clients. You try calling back. The young women employed in liter-ary agencies for the sole purpose of protecting the Agent from the unwanted attentions of her clients now begin fending you off. They'll say she's in a meeting. "But I just spoke to her, a minute ago, we were cut off," you point out, trying to impress the latest bodyguard with the fact that the Agent actually knows who you are and has even gone so far as to call you up—but even as you speak the event has passed into the oblivion of unrecorded history, your name has been forgotten, and though you will phone daily at first, then every hour, there will never be a time when the Agent isn't in a meeting, out for lunch/breakfast/drinks, at the dentist, at a funeral, in China or in California, negotiating an earthquake for one of her Harmony clients. You abandon hope, you send out your last stories along with SASE's to the little mags (payment: one copy, or approximately the cost of postage), and resign your-self to the half-year wait until the story comes back with a printed rejection slip confounded by a few handwritten words above the illegible signature saying this is Marvelous! splendid writing! or *really* good! You might send it out again for more of the same; more likely, you file it away in the by now ludicrously captioned "works in progress" file and tell whoever asks that you've gone into early retirement. Then one day the phone will ring and a vaguely familiar voice will say, "There's an editor at *Redbook* you should talk to. I've told her about your idea for a piece on malaria and she wasn't interested, but you might want to explore some other possibilities."

At this point you will perhaps venture to ask what it had been that she'd told you to drop everything for a few months back. You will hear the frown in her voice, feel her eyes moving over the contracts piled on her desk, and then your heart skips a beat as she says carelessly, "Too bad you never followed that up. We got a $2.7 million advance for it from Knopf. Make sure that proposal gets to me by Friday. Send it Federal Express," she says. "Bye, sweetheart."

"Proposal? What proposal?" you scream into the dead phone, knowing in that instant that you will have to take up fencing again, with Stacey and Gina and Mona and Laverne and all the young women who waft through the office, college diplomas still wet behind their ears, as they spell themselves for several months before drifting upward into the empyrean of publishing or vanishing forever into the clouds of their own literary aspirations. None of these Sues and Sallys know the names of the authors the Agency represents (certainly they don't know yours), and they've never heard of anything you've written even though your publications are loyally displayed on the shelves in the foyer along with the other books that have been published by the grace of the Agent's intervention; and if it should ever happen that a check comes in to the office for you, they'll send it to an address of a place you once stayed in for two weeks in summer thirteen years ago and which burned to the ground a week later. Or they'll send your check to someone else. To these Janes and Josies all authors are the same.

I've received checks for Monika Milliken as well as for Albert Vox, but because bank clerks are more discriminating than people who work in literary agencies, I've never been able to cash any of them.

But you re-enter the fray, take up again the almost hopeless task of getting through the barricade of Rebeccas and Randi Sues in an attempt to discover what proposal you're supposed to have in by Friday. Once again, the Agent is inundated by important visitors from emerging nations, endless meetings and a series of calamities both personal and cosmic; and when, after many years of this, you decide finally to fire your agent, there's no possible way to inform her of your intention. You can't get through directly, of course, which is why you decided to fire her in the first place, and leaving a message with one of the disembodied young voices would be an act of cowardice, and also tacky. Besides, you're reasonably sure the message would never be relayed. A cardinal rule in literary agencies stipulates that Bad News is No News. If your work has been rejected, you're the last to know, and you can remain in limbo for months and even years before a surge of housecleaning at the Agency brings you news that your manuscript was unfortunately "lost"—a supposedly kind way of letting you know it was never worth receiving to begin with.

You decide to write a letter; you're a writer, after all. You've had it, you write, this time you mean it: good-bye, *finito,* and no *au revoir.*

You tear it up: too strident. The next is weak—why should you be apologizing, after all?—and the one after that too curt. The day goes by, drafts blanket the floor. The cat makes ominous scratching movements in the papers at your feet. You tell it to go; you don't need a critic. The cat looks at you with deep sorrow and bolts out the door. But finally, you get it right, the letter's perfect, *le mot juste* in every phrase. You address the envelope, affix a stamp and drive down to the post office to make sure it goes out first thing in the morning. You wait.

You picture her face when she receives it. Her look of alarm as she tears open the envelope, sensing something wrong—no, she opens it cautiously, fearing a bomb inside. She reads, gasps, and reaches for the phone. Overcome with remorse, she begs you for another chance. She begs for mercy. And you will show it to her, like gentle rain from heaven. You will understand that the fault was not hers, it lay in the incompetencies of the Lucys and Listas and Lolly Maes, but they've all left, thank God and the Devil take them, and there's nothing to come between the two of you ever again.

Days pass, the leaves fall, a cold wind brings the snow. Nothing. Not a sound, not the slightest rustle, and the telephone never brings her voice. Thanksgiving is here—but what is there to be thankful for? Christmas is coming, and a new year will begin. It is time to set out on the sad quest for another agent.

You wander through the labyrinthine ways, going from one to the other with Kafka as your guide and *Catch-22* as their catechism. If you were really a writer, you'd have an agent already. You wouldn't be here.

I had one, you explain, fourteen long years, but in the end I had to fire her.

Since when does a writer fire an agent?

I had to, you see, I could never get in touch with her.

If you couldn't be satisfied with Melody Krassner, you certainly wouldn't be happy with us. (A shrug of the shoulders: as if we'd have you.) Good bye, good luck.

It happens I did have luck. Quill & Pepper Inc., the agency that had represented me in the days of my precocity when I first returned from England was willing to take me back. Unlike the tiny fiefdom of Melody Krassner, Quill & Pepper was a large sprawling agency, its tentacles or pseudopods reaching far beyond the world of print. It was ruled by many, not one, the separate agents each tending to his own flock or diocese with no visible interference from above. My agent had been a man in his eighties, very tall with a shock of white hair, who had died shortly after my fourth novel was published and it was not held against me when I left him on this account.

They took me back *in caritas,* for old time's sake, and Joellen Crim, formerly of Subsidiary Rights, became my agent. She was a woman who looked as though she'd passed her prime before she was out of college and had been aging ever since. But she was solicitous and maternal (in the manner of childless women who have never felt betrayed by their offspring); she invited me to her apartment, inquired after the health of my family and sometimes gave signs of a buried though still vital humor. "As my grand-mother used to say," she would begin, her eyes growing large with the merriment to follow, "As my grandmother used to say"—lips trembling with suppressed laughter—"we must all try to live like the Poets, dear—Byron and Shelley." Then she laughed till the tears came, a joke on old grandmother: what a crew they were, those Romantics, how classic their incest.

She showed her dedication by sending off again, on the very day it was returned, whatever piece of mine had been rejected. Though I sometimes questioned her judgement in deciding where to send what (*Penthouse,* for instance, didn't strike me as a likely market for a proposed article on the history of coffee and coffee houses, nor did *The New Yorker* seem the perfect choice for a piece on the bestiality of Catherine the Great), there was no doubting her sincerity or her devotion. With Joellen Crim as my agent, I was no longer forgotten, though I was in danger of being well-meaninged out of existence.

When the phone rang on the 26th of October and the Voice from My Past said, "Write down this number," I was no less dumbfounded than if I'd been Macbeth, hearing that Birnam Wood advanced on Dunsinane.

"Richard Gernreich. He needs a writer to collaborate on a commercial novel. You'd be perfect."

I didn't think I'd still be feeling it, the pangs of separation, the crazy sense of abandonment, the rupture once again; the loss. It was no better—in fact, just the opposite—for knowing she hadn't noticed anything. To go through separation and divorce with a partner who remains oblivious of the fact could be more terrible, I was now realizing, than the scenes and recriminations. It showed that I didn't exist, and perhaps had never really existed for her, at all.

"The outline's been sold to Harrier for six figures. You get fifty percent. I told him you were a classy writer and you can write wall-to-wall, the way you did your last ghosting job. He's waiting for your call. Let me know what happens."

Click. Dial tone.

Sweet Malady, for all your sins forgiven.

II

VINES

"Judith Krantz got \$3 million for *Princess Daisy*, but I don't think we should ask for that until our fourth novel."

"It might seem greedy," I acknowledged. Through open shutters, slabs of sunlight fell like butter on the kitchen table. We were drinking mugs of coffee, a basket of fresh rolls set between us.

"It's not that," Gernreich said. "Pubbubbub . . . " He was attempting to ingest his croissant whole, like a snake a mouse. Muffled sounds followed his experiment; then he swallowed, pale with satisfaction. "Publishers just aren't giving out that kind of money these days."

I nodded. It was a known fact to anyone who read the book pages that the unprecedented three-million-dollar sale of Krantz' third novel, bought at auction, had produced a series of violent aftershocks in the publishing industry. Few houses could expect to remain solvent in the wake of such catastrophic competition, and the aftermath of *Daisy* had forced many small and independent publishers to go under.

"But that's temporary. Four years from now, they'll be begging us to take it. Knightsbridge'll be on top of the heap by then, Harrier doing anything to keep us." He poured what remained of the coffee into our mugs and got up to make another pot.

I'd been here nearly an hour and a half already and so far we hadn't even mentioned the outline I'd come to discuss. Mainly, he'd talked about Knightsbridge, how he'd conceived her and brought her into being. I didn't object; it was pleasant enough, listening to his stories of creation (Jupiter describing the birth of Minerva) while sitting in his kitchen, a bright, cheerful room, old-fashioned in expanse and up-to-date in efficiency. It was the kind of kitchen I wouldn't have minded having myself, preferably in my house in the south of France, with self-cleaning Mediterranean breezes. White wooden cupboards lined the upper walls, hung above white counters where labor-saving machines designed in Italy and executed in Germany stood ready to chop, slice, grind, sharpen or process into another form. The mustard-patterned linoleum on the floor was shining as if placed in perpetual care with Mr. Clean. Evidences of a family life were tacked on the bulletin board or held by cute magnets to the refrigerator door: clipped coupons, Things to Buy, hurried messages jotted on scraps of paper, their brevity making them urgent and intimate: "Rich, call Bonnie abt. Sat. nite"; "P. L. arr. TWA 647 1:15 JFK"; "Dr. Luger—3 P.M. Wed."; and the mysterious: "What about Iggy?"; in addition to the usual children's scrawls brought home from school in proud though dubious testimony to artistic talent.

Gernreich set the coffee going and came back to the table.

"Four years, five at the most. Knightsbridge will definitely be into seven figures by then."

It was time, I thought, to broach the subject of our meeting. "About *Vines . . .* " I began.

"The second Knightsbridge will knock their socks off. It takes on heart surgery. The surgeon's a redhead, born in Rome in a grubby little palazzo. She's a street urchin, like Sophia Loren in— what was that movie? Where she's a baker's daughter?" He cupped his hands several inches in front of his chest, palpating the air. "Magnificent. It's called *Hearts.* The third will be about . . ."

"You can't," I interrupted. "*Hearts* has been used." It was the title of a novel by Hilma Wolitzer, then recently released in paperback.

"Doesn't matter. Titles can't be copyrighted. You could use *Hamlet* if you wanted to. Anyway, people forget what they read." Delicately, he lifted the crumbs from his plate with a moistened fingertip and flicked them into his mouth. "The third will be about a producer. She gets to be the richest woman in the world. The whole movie industry from way back when. It's called . . . "

"*Takes?*"

"Not bad." He gave me the closed-lip smile of a teacher obliged to acknowledge effort on the part of a student. "But it doesn't convey the elusive quality of films, their magic, the dream of escaping into the screen. I thought of *Projections*—though that might be too complicated. Maybe just the heroine's name: *Magda.* She was born in Hungary, in Budapest, during the uprising."

"Of 1956?"

"Whenever."

"She's awfully young to be so rich."

"She's a genius is why."

I played with the edge of the yellow legal pad containing my notes. The conversation was making me extremely nervous. What little I knew about wines was encyclopedic compared to my knowledge of the other subjects. About heart surgery I knew nothing at all. About surgery of any kind, and about medical matters in general, I was far less informed than the average twelve-year-old whose TV diet included doctor-and-hospital soaps. The kind of prurience appealed to in "General Hospital" or "General Delivery" or "I.V. & Stat" left me unmoved. Though I'd played Doctor as a child and remembered liking it (the game, I believe, consisted of pulling down your pants and having your temperature taken—or doing it to someone else), I'd long since lost interest and could now not remember either my blood pressure or type or whether it had been German measles or chicken pox I'd had in the third grade. As for film-making, I was equally hopeless. Against the spate of Hollywood novels, the expertise of people who took courses at the New School, or of those who frequented theaters called cinemas and sat through the entire works of directors with names like Xerxes or Suomi or Anaconda, I was as a newborn babe, a *tabula rasa,* a throwback from the world of print.

"And the fourth book?" I asked recklessly. Maybe we would have an astronaut by then, or a quantum physicist, a brunette, specializing in left-spinning neutrinos and charmed or colored quarks.

"Can't let the cat out of the bag all at once, that spoils the fun." He winked and stood up. The black Braun electric coffee maker on the counter had come to the end of its cycle. "We need our secrets," he said royally as he went to get it, adding: "Good title, that."

"Secrets?"

"I've a feeling it's been used though."

"But you said . . . "

"I mean by somebody really big. Danielle Steel maybe. There's time though. All I can tell you is the fourth will probably be real estate. Or horses." He poured thoughtfully. "There's more romance to horses, but houses are a good bet too, especially if we have a heroine like Leona."

"Helmsley?"

"Right. Though we'd have to disguise her, of course. Make her younger, give her light-colored hair. A blonde again, or maybe even premature gray? Silver, white . . . that's it! a young woman with white hair can be a knockout. Snow White and the gnomes. She'll be a queen though, standing guard. We'll give her a palace. Palace, *Palaces*—great title." He reached for the last of the croissants, this one chocolate-filled. "Excuse me," he said and, carrying the roll between his teeth like a cat bearing off a rodent before it snaps the neck, Gernreich strode toward the bathroom.

He returned about ten minutes later and asked if I'd care to have some lunch. It could wait, I said. I held up my legal pad meaningfully. There were certain things we had to talk about first.

Such as what?

The outline. There were several points that troubled me . . .

For instance?

"The part where our heroine is born in a manger on Christmas Day."

"What about it?"

"I can't do it."

"No?" He sucked on his upper lip. "It's a good touch, that. Dramatic."

"But I'm Jewish!" It wasn't what I meant to say, that wasn't the point, but the words spilled out before I could stop them.

He nodded pleasantly: isn't everyone?

"I mean, it isn't a scene I feel I could write."

"Other people have been born that way."

"Only one, as far as I've heard—and that's exactly the problem." He deliberated for a moment. "I think I see what you're getting at," he conceded. "Would it make things easier if it wasn't Christmas?"

"Much easier." My sense of relief at that moment caused me to smile and nod my head so vigorously that, though I didn't yet realize it, I was from then on compromised, and her birth, though it would be moved to an earlier season, would have to take place in a manger.

I couldn't then argue with her name either. "Fleur de mon coeur!" her father cries out upon her delivery, before his voice is drowned in a blast of gunfire, and Fleur she remains. Though V assured me it could be worse—she had a relative named Tansy Two and a goddaughter Clytemnestra ("Clyt" for short)—I found the name egregious. Who could identify with a heroine named Fleur? Rose was fine, or Daisy (Marguerite in French). Lily or Laurel would do, Heather or Holly: even Poppy was better. I'd known a woman called Periwinkle when I lived in England and she was perfectly charming. But Fleur? Why not Legume in that case, or Bush? It was too soon, however, to be quibbling with nomenclature; there were more crucial matters to deal with first.

Lactation, for one. The heroine's birth is followed almost immediately by the aforementioned blast of gunfire and burning of the manger (to permit the untimely but plot-essential death of poor Fleur's mother), and her father, Phillipe de Bousquet, being pursued by Nazi collaborationists, snatches his newborn from the devouring flames and makes off with her to the dark virgin woods where they will remain in hiding for the space of several months, or until liberation into the following chapter.

"Phillipe would have to lactate," I pointed out.

"How's that?"

"He can't keep Fleur alive unless he does." (I didn't bother to bring up the problem of cold nights in the deep woods at this point; if need be, Phillipe could bundle her in leaves or straw, or skin a sheep for baby bunting.) "He can't be heating up formulas in the wilderness."

Gernreich narrowed his eyes in astonishment. "Lactation," I insisted. "Either the father lactates or the woods have got to go."

He'd obviously given no thought to the matter until now, and he began improvising frantically. "We'll skip that part, go straight from the burning manger to when they're already living in town. When he's working as a cooper. Nobody'll notice."

I stood my ground. "They will."

"She'll be eating solid food by then," he pleaded.

"No." I was merciless. "Doesn't matter." I reminded him of what he'd told me earlier, that eighty-five to ninety percent of readers would be women. Of these, I now estimated, not less than sixty-five percent would have lactated at some point in their lives, were currently lactating, or were expecting to lactate in the future. Those readers, I pointed out, would definitely notice that something was missing.

"But this is a novel! It's fantasy, invention . . . "

"Babies who can live on air?"

"Well," he said and, "Well," again. He stood up and repeated it a third time. "There may be something in what you say." He began walking out of the kitchen. "Give me a few minutes, I'll work it out."

I didn't doubt that he would find a solution, if not a formula. Already, only three days after our first meeting, and despite having read the outline, I recognized a kind of genius in Gernreich. He was a mad inventor, an inspired designer of plots, whose flair for the expected was of no less brilliance than the startling innovativeness of Rudi Gernreich (no relation), designer of the topless dress, whose accomplishments raised to the very peak of fashion the exposed breasts of the middle to late sixties. Though Rudi's artistry was expressed through what might be seen as a negative capability (precursor of minimalism?), Richard's lay in acts of commission. He came from the school of "More is More," as indicated by the outline.

It was rich in deed. The 203 pages abounded in plot, subplot and counterplot, deceptions and vituperations—revenge he did particularly well—hopes dashed and raised again, burning vineyards (not only the manger succumbed to the flames), attempted rape and the loss of virginity, forgeries, bacchanals, deaths violent and lingering—and through it all, like a golden river washing the valley where the grapes are grown, ran the bubbling dream of fair-haired Fleur as she rode the currents toward the mouth of her success.

In style of workmanship, Richard was Rudi's antithesis. Though both Gernreichs were after the same ends (eponymous with their name), Richard was the Picasso to Rudi's Braque. His work reached in many directions. In addition to Knightsbridge, Richard had several other authors, a stable of writers who, lured by his carrot of promised wealth, had until now provided his bread and butter.

But now he longed for champagne. He had conceived Jacqueline Knightsbridge out of that longing and had created her to be a cut above the others. She was to be his triumph, a thoroughbred among the workhorses, and already he was grooming her for the Stakes.

He'd chosen (or designed) her name with care, he'd explained earlier this morning, after considerable market research in book stores, supermarkets, any kind of store where books were sold. Since novels are arranged alphabetically by author, and since "most people buy what's directly in front of them on the shelves when they come in," Gernreich had decided to christen his author somewhere in mid-alphabet, where she would get the most exposure and the most sales.

From J to M, or thereabouts (James to Kafka to Lawrence to Melville) represented the bibliographic equivalent to *Playboy's* centerfold: the place to be, where the action was. "The center of the alphabet, that's where you sell."

"Which must be why Jane Austen and Emile Zola never made it," I said, regretting it immediately. There was no point biting the hand, after all. Gernreich was the owner and trainer of Knightsbridge, the producer to my subcontractor (if I should get the job). There were many more like me around, but only one of him.

He had, in fact, fired the writer who'd been working with him originally. After about three hundred pages, he'd realized she didn't have the "magic" he intended for Knightsbridge—"she couldn't put out the way I wanted"—and he'd let her go. It was then four months after the signing of the contract, only eight months away from deadline for submission of the completed novel. He needed a new writer fast and turned again to his agent (Malady) to bring forth another. This being New York City, unemployed writers were considerably easier to find than the Aztec virgins demanded for their routine sacrifices; I knew I was only one of many possible candidates on Malady's list. But my ability to write wall-to-wall, as she called it, and my European background, which she conveniently mistook for "classiness," not to mention my "expert" knowledge of wines, had all qualified me as her first choice among the contenders for Knightsbridge.

Happily, Gernreich ignored my comment on writers at the extremities. "Also," he continued, "I wanted a name with real class to it." The primary requisite was centricity; after that, he'd sought a name that rang of aristocracy, of royalty if possible. "King," the obvious choice, had already been usurped by Stephen. A Kingsley on the best-seller list at the time ruled out that possibility, and Kingston didn't work because of the town. Queen, Prince, Duke and Earl were all too far off-center, and Marquis was too foreign. Knightsbridge had come to him as an inspiration, carrying with it "a certain aura" that was better than Knight alone. The first syllable brought a connotation of nobility and legend; the "bridge" made it solid. Together, they combined into a name that was both glamorous and traditional, London's wealthiest shopping district, home of Harrod's and of Christine Keeler (a call girl who brought down the government in the Profumo scandal of the sixties), a name richly endowed with privilege.

Her Christian name came to her afterwards, though preceding Knightsbridge in sequence. "It's good when the initials of the two names follow each other in alphabetical order," he told me. "K follows J."

I thought it unnecessary to protest my mastery of the alphabet at this point. A few days earlier I would have thought such a skill to be prerequisite to the writing of novels, or of anything else for that matter. I knew my ABC's and I knew them perfectly, but I repeated, like a willing apprentice, "K follows J," though I could see no reason for the sequencing.

"There isn't any," he admitted, and for a moment he seemed almost endearing. "I just like it—and who knows? it might be lucky." The rabbit's food of blockbusting fiction? I wondered. "Anyway, it's worked before. Take Judith Krantz."

We always came back to her, it seemed. Like the roads of France, marked "Toutes Directions," it didn't matter which one you took, since all of them eventually led to the same place, which was called "Centreville."

"Or Charles Dickens," he went on, abandoning the center, "Gaylord Hauser, Henrik Ibsen, Robert Louis Stevenson—if you take away the Louis." He shrugged. "Anyway, J names are magic for women authors: Jacqueline Susann, the Collins sisters, Jean Auel."

He'd toyed with Jayne, too tacky with the "y," too plain without it; with Johanna, but that brought Heidi to mind, and the grandfather and the Swiss Alps; and for a few days he'd seriously considered Jocelyn. It was Anglo, to go with Knightsbridge, and refined enough for anyone, but there was something lubricious about the name, and possibly snotty besides. Jackie was good, but a little too jaunty and too masculine in print. The longer version was better. Just right, in fact, combining a class act (as in Kennedy or Onassis), with a hint of sex (via Bisset) and best-sellerdom (via Briskin, author of the minimalist classic, *Everything and More*). Jacqueline coupled with Knightsbridge like John with Keats: a magnetic symbiosis.

I heard a shuffling sound and a moment later Gernreich came back into the kitchen. Instead of the sneakers he'd had on before, he was now wearing oversize fur slippers and his feet, lodged in them marsupially, scuttled across the linoleum like a pair of wombats.

Another form of rabbit's foot, I wondered? He was smiling shyly. "It came to me," he admitted. "Phillipe doesn't make off with her into the woods after all. There's this Mother Superior, disguised as a soldier. When the manger bursts into flame she tears the baby out of his arms. She runs. Phillipe can't follow her, of course, he's got these Nazis coming after him, so he flees into the night on his own."

"Meanwhile"—he was pacing as he talked, the susurrations of his slippers playing a soft accompaniment to his words—"the baby's brought to the local orphanage, where the nuns take care of her. They nurse her with their milk. After a few months or so— however long it takes to get her off their breasts—Phillipe comes back for her. It's the dead of night. He steals into the orphanage, climbs up the twisting boughs espaliered against the wall until he's at the third-floor window. He opens the sash quietly, creeps into the room. The children are sleeping. They're in cribs lined up one next to the other. He searches their faces. For a moment he's frightened. He can't find her—she's gone, he thinks, they've taken her away. But then he sees her. She opens her eyes, her lids are delicate as petals—Fleur, you know? flower?" I nodded acknowledgment of the conceit. "He lifts her gently from the crib and she doesn't make a sound. Just looks at him. He cradles her in his arms, it's as if she knows what's happening."

Gernreich was flushed, his eyes no longer muddy, bright as jellybeans now. "He carries her down through the tangled boughs. His arms are cut and bleeding, but she's miraculously unscathed. When they're on the ground, he runs, faster than he's ever run before, even from the soldiers"—he gave me a quick look—"spurred by hope this time, not fear."

"Right," I said.

"He goes on running until the orphanage is nothing but a tiny speck in the distance. Until even that fades, and they're safe. They're free!"

He sat down, triumphant. I didn't know what to say. "It's . . . it's . . . very good, Richard."

"Call me Rich. It's brilliant, is what it is. Much, much stronger this way. The father kidnapping his own child! Great—and it would've never happened without you." He blinked as if he were a television genie who'd conjured me by accident. "I wouldn't have thought of it if you hadn't brought up that point about nursing."

I blushed. "It's nothing."

"It's terrific. We get to keep everything we had before, and the kidnapping on top of it! That's the way I like to work. Give and take, creative feedback. Get into the reader's head. That's why I need input from a woman's point of view. Knightsbridge's got to see things like a woman—if I didn't know that, I'd be writing her myself."

Encouraged by the praise, I asked how Phillipe was able to recognize his child.

"Well, he'd have to, his own flesh and blood."

"In the middle of the night . . . ?"

"We'll hang a full moon, give him a flashlight."

I was again struck by his audacity, the sheer chutzpah of the little man, who could raise the moon as lantern and feed a child on the milk of nuns. But even so. "He's seen her only once, for a few seconds at birth, and all newborns look pretty much the same. How does he pick her out from among all the other babies many months later?"

"She's his own kid, after all . . . "

"Blood won't tell."

"He'll feel something . . . "

"Are you sure that's being fair to the reader?"

Like a red flag to a bull, the question set him into action. He was thinking furiously, I could tell, his head tilted to the right, charging the obstacle with the left, logical side of his brain. "We need a sign, a birthmark, something he could notice even when she's being born. Nothing disfiguring, of course. Something tiny and distinctive, a touch of something. *A Touch of Venus,* what was that about? Doesn't matter, a slight imperfection that adds beauty to the whole, like the Greeks said. When she's older it can be something her lover goes wild about, on her chest, maybe, near her heart like a delicate tattoo, rose-colored, a strawberry mark . . . "

"*Tâche de vin.*"

"What's that?"

"*Tâche de vin.* It's French for 'strawberry mark.'"

"You're kidding!" He stared. "It's just what we need, the 'touch of wine.' Destiny, imprinted on her breast. As though the gods had kissed her there. Of course Phillipe would notice that first thing. It's perfect."

"It's nothing," I said again, though I felt a peculiar pride, as if my simple translation from English to French had been the Open Sesame into the fabulous wealth of his imagination.

"They're going to love you at Harrier," he said. "Tachdyvin— what a team we're going to make!"

Though Gernreich assured me I was the writer he was looking for, the final say remained with Harrier. The publishers would have to agree to the amending of their contract with "Knightsbridge," who represented the collaboration of Gernreich and the original writer. My name would then be substituted for hers, the terms remaining the same, the monies to be paid equally to both parties. For that to be effected, we needed the approval of Winnie Silver, Harrier's Publisher and Editor-in-Chief.

Gernreich had arranged a meeting with her on the following Tuesday at ten. "You've got nothing to worry about," he said as I placed the outline and notes into my briefcase, preparing to leave. We'd been together for nearly four hours and I was acutely aware that he was overdue for lunch.

"Forget it," he said magnanimously, waving me back to my seat. "I can eat anytime." He looked at his watch. "Well, just a few minutes, a quick briefing."

I sat down again. "Don't worry," he repeated. "I'll do most of the talking anyway. All you have to do is tell her how you're really thrilled about this project, you know it's going to be terrific, a blockbuster, sure-fire, guaranteed success."

"But . . . "

"You might throw in something about that wine cellar, you know—how your father was a big investor in wines" (he wasn't), "and you grew up learning all about them" (I hadn't) "and how you're something of an expert . . . "

"I'm not."

Gernreich shrugged. "Who's to know? Tell her you can't wait to get started on the book. You're sure it'll make millions, tell her. Make her feel good about it, you know."

My throat constricted. I'd never remember the lines, I was sure.

"The important thing is talking it up. People in publishing, most of them don't have time to read, so basically they're insecure about the books they buy. You got to reassure them, make them feel they did the right thing."

Reassure *them*? This talk was giving me a serious attack of stage fright. How could I possibly act the part he'd assigned to me? I was only a writer, after all, not a literary performance artist. I asked how my predecessor had fared at the auditions.

"Fine. I talked her up, told them she was great. They approved."

"And after the first 300 pages—what did they think then?"

"I never showed them the manuscript. No point—it might have discouraged them."

"Why?"

"Boring, that's why. Worst thing possible for a best-seller to be. Boring is death."

"What did she do wrong?"

"Had a baby." He walked over to the refrigerator and took out a solid brown object the size of a small log. "Nothing I could do to stop it. She was having personal problems with her husband and she wanted a child." He placed what appeared to be the leg of a young mammal inside the microwave to incubate. "I told her not to, at least not until she'd finished *Vines*. I knew it would be a distracting influence. But she had to have it her own way, she went ahead with the baby."

He turned and came toward me. "I had no choice, you see. I

had to let her go before she killed the book." He smiled suddenly. "But why talk about past history? It's got nothing to do with us. You," he said, eyeing me carefully as I started for the door, "don't have any personal problems, do you?"

"Of course not," I assured him and hurried out.

The Agent: Crim

The cucumber slice had long since sunk to oblivion in the milky depths of the vichyssoise when we finally sat down to dinner. Joellen enjoyed fussing with a meal. To her, preparation was the best part. The skinning, peeling, stuffing, blanching, all belonged in the realm of expectation, foreplay to the act itself, a long time coming, and of only minor interest compared to the stages that led up to it. She attended to the details, leaving the composition of the meal to take care of itself. Dinners cooked by Joellen were never orchestrated, the side dish ignorant of the main dish's theme. Though Melody Krassner could achieve harmony for some of her authors, Joellen Crim, in her nurturing kindness, dished out cacophony to all.

It was Monday night, eve of my meeting at Harrier. The weather had turned suddenly cold, and the chilled vichyssoise was no more devoutly to be wished than a steaming bowl of *goulaschsuppe* in mid-August. But by the time we came to eat it, the soup had stabilized at room temperature. Neither hot nor cold, it had lost all distinctiveness and was now simply an inoffensive, though doubtless well-meaning comestible.

I'd decided to wait until we were at the table before broaching the subject of my disloyalty. (I'd originally invited her out to dinner by way of preliminary recompense, but she'd refused. "A waste of money," she'd said sensibly—she was always sensible; that was the essential Crimness about her—"I have food at home and no one to eat it with, so come have dinner with me.") I'd had to accept, though I was regretting it now.

We were sitting opposite each other at the round dining table in an alcove off the living room, silverware gleaming in candlelight, blue islands of shadow pulsing across the tablecloth. Candles in silver holders. Silver in the morning. I had to tell Joellen, and I wished for the protective neutrality of a public eating place, interrupted by waiters, distracted by floating scraps of conversation from neighboring tables. Instead we were dining at a table for two in the redundant privacy of her garden alcove, potted with plants to create a recess of nature set back from the wall of books that lined the whole of her apartment. Books spilled from living room to kitchen, out along the corridor, making a small inroad into the bathroom and out again down the hall to her bedroom. It was a serious library. In the living room alone the shelves contained the complete works of Freud and James (both of them), all of Balzac's *Human Comedy,* the letters of Chekhov, a section devoted to philosophy and religion, another to drama, another to the life sciences. Whenever I was in that room, I felt I'd been put into the playpen of western civilization, its greatest thinkers surrounding me like a wall of nannies.

We'd had drinks there and in the kitchen (where bookshelves contained a lighter fare: cookbooks and novels), our peripatetics tuned to the cry of the timer. Now we were *hors d'oeuvres,* seated to the side of the volumes in our bastion of wilderness, about to start dinner. Joellen was rosy with her exertions, her skin flushed at the neck of a tangerine silk blouse she'd put on for the occasion, matching the small cameo she'd inherited from her grandmother. A bottle of excellent Alsatian Riesling stood uncorked in the silver wine cooler. She'd obviously put herself out for our dinner, and the sad spectacle of our intended festivity drove my guilt to the region of my larynx, making me hideously polite and nearly incoherent as I praised the settings first and then the soup.

Rosencrantz and Guildenstern! Smiling, I lowered the spoon to the soup. Smiling, I raised it to my lips and swallowed. It is set down that one may smile, and smile, and be a villain. I knew I had

to tell Joellen and I had to tell her now. But how should I begin?
The silver spoon shuttled from bowl to mouth. Even if Silver
rejected me in the morning, or if, despite Harrier's approval,
Gernreich would fire me soon after; or if in the end it was I who
decided not to do it, still I had to let Joellen know what was afoot.
It was only right—after all, Joellen had taken me on when no one
else would have me. She'd nurtured me in her fashion. It wasn't
her fault that I'd picked up the telephone that day and hearkened
to the siren call of Malady, though she'd be sure to learn about it
sooner or later—certainly sooner if I signed the contract tomorrow
—and I didn't want the news to come to her by way of the unfeel-
ing (though in this case perhaps appropriate) grapevine.

I wanted to apologize first, explain later. I wanted her forgive-
ness before the confession. I wished we'd gone to a restaurant.
Most of all, I wished I were home and in bed and didn't have to
say anything to anybody about this ever again. I was worn out by
it. Repelled by what I was drawn to—though that didn't describe
it accurately either, since the two sensations were never present
simultaneously. At the end of last Thursday's meeting with
Gernreich, when he'd assured me that publishers don't read and
that I'd be called upon to perform according to hype, I felt as I
had when first looking upon his outline, and I'd rushed out of the
kitchen, out the door and down the steps, telling myself that never
would I be so needy that I'd be forced to engage in literary acts of
such unmitigated vulgarity; that if ever I decided to prostitute
myself, it would be in the straightforward way and not through
words. On the streets I was accosted by the goblins of my panic;
demons approached me from behind. Was he driving me mad
already? Ghoulies and ghosties—ahead of me, a small ghost was
stepping off the curb into the face of oncoming traffic. I shouted
out a warning and, as she retreated to the sidewalk, the monsters
blended into children, carrying paper bags for trick or treat. It was

the 31st of October. With Becky in her teens now, at an age when outright disguise would threaten the many costumes of her changing identity, and the twins long grown, I'd forgotten Halloween.

In the car I kept the windows closed and turned the radio on loud. Country music—Waylon, Willie and the boys . . . In the tunnel the radio crackled and died, beyond the range of waves. I've always disliked tunnels, not because I see them in a Freudian way, as vaginal passage, expulsion from the womb; to me they're claustrophobic, bringing visions of suffocation and watery death: the city's underbelly, a large intestine snaking out from Manhattan to empty its waste in the boroughs. But I'd learned to live with them over the years; like someone whose fear of flying is never conquered, though it dissipates through lack of alternatives, I drove the tunnel regularly now, the shortest way home.

The music came on again as I rounded the last bend before the mouth (or anus) leading to the tolls. A country boy will survive . . . That was Bocephus, Hank Williams' son, a good old boy pouring out his heart in a song that had everything in it: racism, jingoism, machismo, the unexamined life, boasting and brawling and self-relying, the unselfconsciousness I hankered for. Inching toward home along the Expressway, I began to recover equilibrium. I turned the volume to blaring and screamed along with Hank Jr.; it was one of my favorites.

Why not? I asked myself when it ended. Why not at least try to do the book? Was I a Sartre or a Sontag, to remain aloof from popular delusions and the madness of crowds? What was wrong with trying, for once in my life, to write a book that anyone could read and a lot of people might want to?

And why had I bolted from Gernreich's apartment like Gulliver pursued by Yahoos? Intellectual repugnance? That could hardly be more serious than a passing cold for someone who had learned by heart the lyrics of songs, Tops of the Pops and the Hit

Parade, since the late forties. What then? Scared of flubbing the Knightsbridge? or was it something deeper, more despicable, a dread that whatever talent I might once have had was now so weak, sickly, near to expiring, that if I turned my attention to anything else, it would go out completely? Lodged with me useless? Was I some kind of exotic plant that lives in darkness waiting for its single bloom once in a lifetime?

Goddamn woman! ain't no use holdin' on to it, thang's gon dry out fore you know it, so why not git on down and do it while you can?

The purpose of Knightsbridge is to entertain, nothing more. No one's expecting the novel to reveal the truth to all men, or even to a few women. Does Bocephus tell me how to live? Does Willy? But I listen to them and they make me feel better. In the gridlock of my days they comfort me with song. Why not Knightsbridge? Why not me?

And besides, as Arthur says: No knowledge stinks.

Or V: You'll never know till you try.

Or a saying of my mother's: *Wass der Bauer nicht kennt, Frist er nicht.* Was I a Bauer, an ignorant oaf who refuses even to taste what he's never eaten?

By the time I was home, I knew I'd keep the appointment with Silver, despite the willies, and I knew I had to tell Joellen about it.

"Joellen," I began, resting my spoon on the plate beside the vichyssoise.

"I know. It's terrible. Too starchy and you can't taste the leek. I certainly wouldn't have any more of it if I were you."

I picked up the spoon dutifully. "It's delicious," I said. She was making things unbearably difficult.

"My God!" She pushed back her chair from the table. "I'm forgetting the wine!"

"Let me." I seized the moment, jumped up and over to the wine cooler, grabbing the bottle by its neck. "There's something I have to tell you . . . "

I told her everything, let it all out in a stream of apologies—my surprise, my shock, at hearing from Malady again—pouring the wine like water, to the brim, and dissembling at the same time: if Harrier offered me the contract I'd turn it down, I said; I'd spurn the Knightsbridge and maintain my fealty to herself.

"That would be foolish," she said. "Of no use to anyone."

Her dear earnestness. She cupped the bowl of the glass in both hands to keep it from spilling. "To you and Jacqueline. I hope she makes you very, very rich," she said, meaning it.

She cleared the soup and brought out the veal marsala with its accompanying vegetables. "What I like is a good read," Joellen said, handing me the bowl of succotash first, the turnips after. "There's nothing better than a good read, though some people try to look down their noses at it." She glanced up toward the impassive spines of Tolstoy, Malraux and other Olympians resting on the shelves. "When *Scruples* came out, I couldn't stop, even in the Ladies room. I turned off the phone that day, had my lunch sent in and didn't do a damn bit of work." She smiled in the memory of her debauch. "A wonderful read, don't you think?"

I shrugged. I hadn't read it but, like a cynic impervious to value, I knew its price. Krantz' first novel: it had made $11 million for its author.

"Now you take Danielle Steel," she continued (157 million copies in print, outselling Shakespeare and possibly the Bible), "I find her too soft when it comes to sex—if it's porn, let it be porn, I say—and sometimes her grammar is, well, somewhat *off,* but she's sincere, she can hold the reader too."

I knew something about Steel, though not her books. Her parents were friends of my parents, her mother the most beautiful woman I'd ever seen, Brazilian and exotic as a brown orchid: Norma. She came upstairs to say goodnight when I was about ten or eleven, prepubescent, overgrown and undeveloped. I poured out my heart; I told her my fears that I'd never be able to get a man. "It's easy," she said. Her voice was dark honey. "I'll tell you the secret." She smiled. "All you have to do is flatter them. Admire a man's tie"—she reached for the invisible silk around my neck, stroking it with her fingertips—"'Where did you find this? It's exquisite.' Or his shirt—ask him who his tailor is." She let go, rippling with laughter. "He'll think you're wonderful. Men fall in love with women who make them think more of themselves."

So do readers. From such stock was raised the world's best-selling novelist.

Joellen offered me more turnips. "James Michener is another one," she said. "He's absolutely spellbinding, even though he goes on a bit much. Harold Robbins has been around forever too, though I've never been able to get past the first few pages of any of his books. A writer who uses "orgasm" as a verb deserves to be unread, wouldn't you agree?"

I couldn't say. I'd never even attempted any of the authors she mentioned. I felt depressed and out of my depths. How could I hope to write what I hadn't read? As ye sow, so shall ye reap. As ye read, so shall ye write. Minor writers imitate, major writers steal. Tell me what a person reads, I'll tell you how she writes.

"His characters are simply not believable. They orgasm two, three times a page, and for no apparent reason. And he gets the details wrong. A full-breasted woman who wears a size 5? a junior size? I confess I once threw a book of his across the room, broke the spine too." She grinned. "But he cheats, you see. He suspends the suspension of disbelief. Irwin Shaw, on the other hand, he's a master . . . "

She brought out the pineapple fool, quivering like jelly. I was bound to fail, I knew it. What giddy optimism had prompted me to set out for an alien world without passport or a sense of where I was heading?

"Don't worry," Joellen said, reading my face in the gloom of candlelight. "You'll do it. I know you can."

I shook my head. Impossible. "I don't know what my reader expects. How can I write for her?"

"Write popcorn," she said sensibly. "That's what everyone wants, you know. Good popcorn."

III

THE TRUTH IN FICTION

A Digression: On Truth

"Toute cette fricasée que je barbouille ici n'est qu'un registre des essais de ma vie,"* Montaigne wrote in his *Essais*, bringing respectability and even honor to the practice of stewing about yourself, or literary self-examination. His essays (the pun is the same in English and French) were his attempts to capture, in a particular form, the truths he discovered in his own reflections. He asked himself at the onset, What do I know? and answered, over nearly twenty years and three volumes, that whatever he knew or

*All this fricasee that I am scribbling here is nothing but a record of the essays of my life. ("Of Experience.")

could hope to know could come only through the idiosyncratic filter of himself: who he was and what had happened to him. Since the universe is objective (unknown to itself), all we can perceive of it is through our senses. Our consciousness. In other words, all knowledge is organic; it proceeds from the self. Who I am, the shape of my body, the society I was born into, will condition what I know and how I come to know it. The Truth has come to all men, yet each acts as if he had a private wisdom of his own. (Heraclitus.) The "private wisdom" is subjective knowledge, the little truth that guides our daily actions. What you do is who you are; who you are is what you think. I am what I eat and the manner in which I digest it.

What's the relevance? V asks. "You, madam, are no Michel de Montaigne." She detests what she calls my "waffle."

Granted, I return. But I am using the greater to illuminate the lesser, a rare conceit, litotes' opposite: Brobdingnag for Lilliput, Montaigne for *moi*.

Why?

Because I too am making an attempt, essaying to render a true account of myself.

"Don't bother," V says. "Fiction is an invention of the real. Nobody cares if something actually happened, so long as it's happening now, on the page. There's no distinction between what was and what could have been. 'He lies like an eyewitness'—that's a Russian proverb. My story is whatever I choose to make of it."

Montaigne wrote: if you say "I lie," and tell the truth, you are lying.

Let's not quibble, I tell her. What I'm setting down here is what happened to me, more or less. In the telling, I'll discover what I mean. It's not like writing *Vines,* you see. I have no outline to follow, no bare bones of plot to flesh; I don't know where the story will lead.

"If I knew what was going to happen in a book," V says, "why would I bother to write it?"

Montaigne didn't set down what he already knew. The act of writing was itself part of the process of discovering what he thought. Like a sculptor who perceives in the stone the form he will bring out from it, Montaigne wrestled with words to make them convey what he was on the verge of articulating. The medium is the message. The brushstrokes and pigmentation *are* the irises and sunflowers of Van Gogh. If I write about what I already know, I'm not creating, I'm transcribing. To write about something is not the same as writing it.

"Very good," she says. (I have that line from her.) "But *Vines* was never meant to be a work of art."

Of course not. It was intended as a product (Content: 100 percent words), manufactured to fill a particular demand. A commodity produced and packaged to suit the consumer's taste.

"So what are you saying?"

Will my readers believe me?

To the Reader:

Perhaps you decided many pages ago that what I'm writing here is an invention. At some point, my narrative became too improbable; you balked. Perhaps it was the Christmas birth—surely an exaggeration, you thought, straining too hard for the dubious honor of blasphemy; or was it when I introduced the character of V?—straining again, you thought; unnecessary to turn her into a hermaphrodite, and in bad taste as well.

Let me assure you now that everything is true as I wrote it.

Gernreich did indeed sell his outline of 203 pages to Harrier, a large publishing house owned by FAT (French American Tobacco), which is in turn owned by Cranshaw, an international holding company, and the plot did indeed call for the birth of our heroine to take place as I've described. Jesus Christ or Holy Shit, but that's the way it was. It's also true that I convinced Gernreich to shift the date, though not the place, and that I was able to prevent Fleur's father from being obliged to lactate.

As for V, she's my closest friend. Was, still is: everyman's everywoman, mon semblable, mon frère, or maybe ma soeur. We met, as I've said, in a bar in New York, when she was still Harry and I was still single, looking for love in all the wrong places as the song would tell it a decade later, though at the time I was just going out for a drink. She was sitting at the bar in an old macintosh, loafers dangling from the tops of her feet like bedroom slippers, and wearing a hat that looked like one of Claes Oldenburg's soft constructions. Neither fedora nor trilby, though suggesting a little of both, it was a hat that proclaimed its essential hatness.

My friend Mike was at the adjacent barstool. Always a gentleman, he stood up when I entered and relinquished his seat. "This is Harry," he said. "Harry, meet Kate."

"What do you call that thing on your head?" I asked by way of greeting. Insolent-cute was the style of flirtatiousness then in vogue.

"Thing? What thing?" Harry looked up, caught sight of the brim and made shooing motions with his hand. "Get off! Get down from there at once!" Taking firm hold of it, he lifted the hat high into the air, releasing a long fall of soft brown curls.

Woman's hair. I was perplexed and discomfited. The voice was deep enough for a man, though not too deep for a woman either. I moved closer, trying to read the sex of my neighbor from the texture of the cheeks, but the light of the bar was too dim, and the macintosh concealed whatever protuberances on the chest might otherwise clue me in.

"Harry's a writer too," Mike said. I could tell he was intrigued. Mike was a collector of people, specializing in oddballs, and the way he was smiling told me he'd found a collector's item in Harry, whatever he was.

"Novels?" I asked.

"You could call them that. Most people don't. I take it philosophically."

I smiled. He reminded me of someone, though I couldn't place him. But I felt the jolt that comes from meeting one's own eyes in an unexpected mirror at the far end of the room.

"Mike was just telling me about you, your success as an infant prodigy."

"Not quite."

"Your first book was set in Eden, he tells me. A novel beginning. 'Call me Ishmael'; 'Stately, plump Buck Mulligan'; 'All happy families are alike but an unhappy family is unhappy after its own fashion.' Beginnings are crucial. *Catch-22:* 'It was love at first sight.' Tell me more."

He was charming, erudite. He complimented me, plied me with questions, holding me captive by my own rhetoric. I stopped trying to figure out his physical particularities; what's in a sex, after all? The person was enchanting. I went on talking, and as night wore on, I grew sexier and more brilliant until I so fascinated myself that I felt it was love.

"You're what Kate needs," Mike observed. "I've always thought what Kate needs most isn't an analyst but an audience."

By closing time, the three of us had become thick as triplets, but Harry asked to take me home alone. Mike bowed, to the inevitable, and arm in arm at approach of dawn, Harry and I walked off together into the sunset.

Now that I've told you the facts of our meeting, I know you're willing to entertain the possibility that V exists. But you want to hear more. You're waiting to get to the crucial part, to the heart—or base—of the matter. You're expecting me to let you in on the anatomical specifics. Why, you want to know, was V born male, "or at least taken for one"? You're asking for data, a description or at least definition of the genitals at birth. The fundamentals: the pudenda, please. And if I were to tell you the child was born with a penis, you'd expect me to fill you in on the details of her later surgery.

But I don't give a fig for that, it isn't relevant to the matter at hand. V was both, male and female, not one or the other. Years ago, when she'd gone from Harry to Venus and was called Dr. Raven by her students (at Brunswick State, where she taught English and American literature), I did ask her the obvious question, the question you might ask if I introduced her to you—not at first meeting, of course, but after a while, when you were beginning to feel relaxed in each other's company—the question left hanging by the ancients, for which Tiresias was punished when he presumed to answer:

Who has more pleasure, the man or the woman?

Best of all is making love to a woman, she said.

To oneself, you mean?

Whatever you say.

It was no different, you see, from what you'd expect if you asked the question during your own lovemaking. Somewhere on the rosy plateau, down a notch from the peak of climax and before the descent to detumescence, when both of you lie warm in the currents of your love, and all the body liquids still are sweet; when the foot that rests on the other's is indistinguishable from it, you'll turn and ask, or you'll wonder aloud, you might even argue: It was better for me. Nothing can top the way I'm feeling, nothing could be greater than this.

A sweet debate follows. Especially if the lovers are young, the dialog will go something like this:

SHE: I wish you could be me . . . I wish I could turn you into a woman so you could feel what it's like.

HE: I wish you could.

SHE: What it feels like when you're making love to me . . . when you're inside . . .

HE: I know, I know.

SHE (surprised): How can you?

HE: I feel it too. I can feel you moving there. I feel . . . sometimes it's as though you were inside of me.

SHE: Really? I didn't know . . . (Pause.) It's amazing, isn't it?

HE (stroking her): A miracle.

SHE (reaching for him): Has anybody ever felt like this, do you think?

HE: Nobody. (Chuckling, nuzzling her ear.) We'll never tell them.

And so on to (Fade).

The point is that V could never say anything to you, or to me, that would make us believe she knew what she was talking about. Just suppose she'd answered, "It's better to be the male." Well, then, we'd want to know why that was, and in which respect, and wasn't it simply because she—I'm forgetting—he happened to have been with a wonderful lover at that particular time? Or because it was a case of love, true love, which is blind and otherwise debilitating to the faculties? Mitigating circumstances, we argue, specificities of the occasion—and if V agreed, we'd be no better off than before, and if she didn't, then we'd be forced to fall back on our own counsel.

Que sais-je? Where does truth lie?

In fiction, says V, obviously. Truth lies in fiction as it does anywhere else. You cannot step in and step out of the same river.
(Heraclitus.) No two siblings have the same parents, not even
twins. We cast our lives as novels in order to make sense of them.

Why not essays? I ask. In his Preface Montaigne wrote:
"Reader, I am myself the matter of my book."

The matter is words, says V.

Tuesday morning I drove in to the city for a breakfast meeting
with Gernreich before going on to Silver's office. Entering the tunnel, I hit the tail end of rush hour and got stuck in traffic. I wondered what Gernreich would do if I were late. If I never showed up
at all. Would he eat his breakfast? Would I suffocate? Despite having resigned myself to the inevitability of underwater passage, it
was hard, sitting in a sealed car at the bottom of the East River, the
enclosing air filled with fumes of exhaust, not to think of disagree-
able subjects. Death, for instance, drowning, time running out.
The line of cars remained blocked at either end (like a parenthesis
buried within a footnote), moving neither towards nor away from.
Being stuck forever, in the long sentence of marriage, or trapped,
in a monumental writer's block.

Once, in a convertible (in my twenties), I drove through the
Lincoln Tunnel and saw Christ hovering near the top on the Jersey
side. Scared out of my wits, I decided I had to become a Christian.

A week later I began taking Instruction at a monastery in
Newark with a young Dominican whose arms were downed with
rough blond hair. We'd met at the Cedar Bar, where a group of us
was sitting around a table after a lecture at N.Y.U. He was drinking double bourbons and water, the sleeves of his cassock falling
back toward his elbows, while a Czech named Ladislav, who
worked for Voice of America, was arguing that sex was the natural
outcome of political and national identity. Since he and I were

both Czechs (in a way; my mother had been born in Prague), he insisted we should mate. But I disliked him politically and sexually. He was ferret-faced, conservative, and smelled of camphor. I preferred to talk of God.

Father Giles was blue-eyed, close to thirty and probably a virgin. He was drinking like the Irishman I wasn't. I asked if I could take Instruction. He didn't think so, at first. I said I'd always been drawn to Christianity, the paintings of the Renaissance, Velazquez' Crucifixion, the iconography, lily and rose. It's not the same, he said, what you're talking about is aesthetics. But in the end he agreed to instruct me and I went regularly to the monastery, every Wednesday, there to feast with my ghostly father on the ecstatic words of Augustine and St. Theresa and Katherine of Sienna, who had sixteen male secretaries and held in her hands the decapitated head of one of them, his blood streaming into her images as she caressed the dead face with her worshiping lips. I was close to converting then, even though my friend Mike, himself a lapsed Catholic, advised me to read Martin Buber instead, and Father Giles tried to tell me that the conversion I had in mind was on the order of currency exchange, taking the coin of religion for literature.

I was, in fact, uneasy about actually making the move. My grandmother, left behind in Prague when my parents emigrated, had been fed into an oven at Auschwitz. So had others in my family, none of whom had committed a greater sin than I in having been born. When Father Giles finally put an end to our meetings, I was disappointed, of course, but also relieved. I was a Jew because of history, and I would remain a Jew, regardless of my beliefs.

The Wednesday after my Instruction had ended, I went to meet Mike in the bar where he introduced me to Harry. Later, as V, she urged me to write about my trips to the monastery and it became a satirical novel called *God and Country,* with a double or triple pun on "country," including the Elizabethan meaning ("Do you think I meant country matters?"—Hamlet to Ophelia, asking to lie in her lap).

That was years ago, before I married, when I lived as I wrote and wrote as I lived. Now, after the long ellipsis that followed marriage, I was hoping to start writing again the way I used to, but moving in another direction this time, away from satire toward the real and the true and the financially rewarding. Instead, I was hopelessly stuck in a line of cars under the river, an unnecessary hyphen, caught somewhere between Queens and Manhattan, past and future, between Arthur and Gernreich.

You don't have personal problems, do you?
Of course not.
No more than others. Karenin's wife, for example, or Madame Bovary.
Arthur was still in bed when I'd left the house this morning, though he'd blown me a kiss and wished me luck. He encouraged me as much as he was able, even though Knightsbridge was as far removed from his world as Dolly Parton from Plato or an elephant from academia. Arthur is a classicist. He and Gernreich came from different spheres; they didn't speak each other's language, and I knew, or should have known, that I'd never be able to translate.

At the beginning: *It was love at first sight.* How shall I tell it?
I fell in love with Arthur the moment I saw him, standing in the doorway of my aprtment, big and handsome, in a craggy way, looking like the barbarian chief of an early Germanic tribe. Delivered to my doorstep; I felt what Ptolmy's daughter must have been feeling, down by the stream when Moses floated up to her.
He spoke; and golden syllables fell from the lips of a Stanley Kowalski. He was a man who—as Dostoyevsky said—if he didn't

exist, would have to be invented. The best of all possible worlds: Brando in *The Wild Ones* and Olivier in *Hamlet,* untamed and polished, eloquent and rough; a Hell's Angel on the outside, a Milton within.

He could stay for only a short while that evening, he later explained, because of the twins, Hera and Clio, who were waiting at home. A father too: all things to woman.

The next time we met he took me dancing. It was a hot night, I was strapless. Along the steaming streets he talked of Socrates; of Homer—I was blind with love. On the dance floor he held me tight against him and spoke no more.

Caught in that sensual music, all neglect
Monuments of unaging intellect.

When the band started playing "I'm in the Mood for Love," I said, "So am I." We went back to my apartment and there made our Eden. In the Fall he proposed. I didn't want to marry yet—too soon, my books, and what about his twins?—but in the end I said yes. Partly, I think now, I believed it would be good material. Most people in the world were married or employed (and some were both). I was neither, and felt I might be lacking experience that would give my works universality. As a novelist, I owed it to my readers. It was better to marry than to earn, and besides, I was in love.

We were happy at first; less so as time went on. It was all experience, though none of it turned into material. "All happy families . . ." Tolstoy was wrong: all marriages are like all marriages. The happy ones become the air we breathe and escape the novelist's attention, while the others go on for years and decades, becoming unhappy or simply less-than-happy as the unforgettable is slowly transformed into the forgotten.

In any case, domestic felicity is no theme for novels, and domestic infelicity has no dramatic purpose, except to set the stage for further action.

The Publisher

The traffic began moving again, propelled by whatever mysterious forces control its flow, and I sailed out to Third Avenue with twenty minutes to go, a breeze.

We had breakfast in a hotel dining room just off Fifth, two blocks from Harrier's offices. The Frog ordered bagels and lox—though I'm getting ahead of myself here. I'm writing from the vantage point of hindsight, long after our collaboration became a fact, and after it came to an end. On that Tuesday morning in early November I probably still thought of him as Gernreich. I can't remember; I'm not sure at what point I began referring to my collaborator as the Frog. The name sort of crept up on me, although in retrospect it seems I never thought of him as anything else.

It wasn't because Gernreich resembled a Frenchman in any way, or because his skin was of an unnatural hue; certainly, I didn't think of him as a prince in disguise. But he reminded me of a frog all the same, and it was sometime early on, though I'm not sure exactly when, that whenever I spoke of him (though not to him, of course), I called him the Frog.

He ordered bagels and lox but I was still digesting Joellen's meal of the night before and couldn't stomach anything more rigorous than coffee. Besides, I was nervous. I handed him the short scene I'd written over the weekend, a few sample paragraphs mainly as a test to myself to see if I was capable of doing the kind of thing I thought he expected. It had seemed all right when I wrote it, but after Joellen's disquisition on the masters of popular fiction, I wasn't at all sure it sounded sincere.

"If you're doing it anyway," he'd said on the phone—though

he'd again assured me it wasn't necessary, he had the faith and Silver had no time to read—"pick a moment of high drama. Take something from the middle of the book, some turning point in the action and make it a hook to pull in the reader. Make it short, make it exciting, leave her panting for more."

I'd chosen a scene *in medias res,* after the vineyard has been set on fire.

Fleur walks through the rubble, disheartened and in tears. It is still dark, not yet dawn. She's surrounded by devastation, everything burned to the ground, her dreams ended, the vines useless. She begins to run, as if trying to escape her fate, and stumbles against something on the ground. She kicks at it, tries to kick it away, but it doesn't move. Whatever has tripped her is rooted to the ground. She bends to look and blinks, unbelieving at first. It is a piece of living vine.

She kneels and touches it. The sun is rising over the valley; a new day is beginning. Fleur strokes the fresh green stalk. She's been given a sign, she knows, and from this stalk she will plant new vines, a new vineyard will rise from the ashes of the old, stronger and more resilient than any in California. She looks up across the burned-out field and instead of blackened rubble, she can see the vines growing, the clusters of grapes ripe for picking.

She got to her feet. She would make it happen.
She was a survivor.

"Terrific," he said when he'd finished reading. "It's got just the right touch."

"You really think so?" I reached over and took a bite from the bagel on his plate.

"Absolutely. The part where she strokes the fresh green stalk—it's subliminal."

Subliminal—I hadn't heard the expression in years. But when

he said it, I realized we were products of the same culture, both in our teens when subliminal advertising had been blinked and beeped into our unconscious, sending messages to the id to instruct the ego: Buy. The brainchild of Ernst Dichter, genius of market research, sublimation was the hottest way to sell in the days before we were jaded on TV, when shrinks were still known as psychoanalysts and no one admitted seeing one any more than they'd confess to having plastic surgery done; when gynecological ailments were usually diagnosed as hysterical and cancer was mainly psychological; when more doctors recommended Chesterfield than any other cigarette, and only some people recognized cigarette smoking for what it really was: the sublimation of oral sex. And lollipops and ice cream cones. When cars were "she's" though they were long, hard and glistening, and everything that projected was penile and everything round was mammary; when phallic erections rose up from the bosom of hills, and a billboard on Picadilly Circus, the year I came there, invited you to "Un-zip a banana."

"Great. Really." He must have felt I was still fishing. "The kind of stuff I'm looking for—should I order you a bagel?"

But there wasn't time, 9:45 already. We paid and left, coming out on the avenue and walking south toward the skyscraper where Harrier had its offices.

"You think Silver will like it?"

"Probably. Don't tell her about it, though."

"What do you mean?"

"Don't show it to her either. It's bad policy. Never offer them more than they're expecting. You don't want them thinking you're overeager."

A number of homeless people were squatting at the entrance, some sitting propped against the wall, others sleeping on flats of cardboard. "Let them do the begging," he continued. "You come in with something already done, it makes them suspicious.

Anything that easy, they think, can't be worth all the money they're paying for it."

We went inside, through the marbled lobby lined with columns. "Suppose she asks?" I persisted. Despite what he'd said about publishers having no time to read, it seemed reasonable to suppose she might want to see something in writing (mine) before committing Harrier's six-figure investment.

"Knowing Silver, it's unlikely." We walked toward the elevators at the rear. "But in case she does, tell her you'll try to get something to her in the next couple of weeks. You mail it Federal Express and she'll think you've done her a terrific favor."

"You mean I wait a few weeks to send her the same pages I have with me right now?"

"Right." The elevator opened its maw like a mouth-breeding fish, disgorging passengers. We entered the cavity with a handful of others and rode up to the 46th floor without speaking. Outside the double glass doors leading to the Executive Offices, he gave me final instructions: "Talk up the book, tell her you can't wait to get started, but don't let her know you've been writing for free."

"Trust me," he added, reading my expression.

"I hadn't realized what a lot of politics goes into something like this," I told him.

"The name of the game." He pulled open the doors and ushered me inside.

The front office was guarded by a receptionist who displayed all the charms of a pit bull. Her eyes growled at our approach, signaling a warning in case we'd come to mark her territory. "May I help you?" she barked, as if "help" were a synonym for "eat."

"We're here to see Ms. Silver," the Frog told her. "Jacqueline Knightsbridge."

"Which one of you is Jacqueline?"

He ignored the question. "We have a ten o'clock appointment."

Cerberus shrugged and, probably sensing that we offered no challenge to her dominance, pressed the intercom. Two minutes later a freshly washed and starched young woman stepped out from behind the sliding doors to lead us crisply through the labyrinth of hallways into Silver's inner sanctum.

The lighting was fluorescent. Miniature fig trees, interspersed with tiny citruses, stood in wooden planters around the room like Japanese toy sentinels or the border of a Gobelin. The walls were hung with enormous constructions of purple and chrome and a black-lacquered conference table stretched like a fashion runway down at the far end. It was not a room so much as a "space," or perhaps an "environment," though not in the sense that Darwin would have recognized. Here, nature and art had been forced to switch categories, the formal topiary of the trees standing in marked contrast to the "natural" art that was allowed to run wild, spreading and taking over the walls like giant fungi.

Winnie Silver stood up when we entered. She was tall and lanky, a perfect clotheshorse who'd been put together by a personal shopper in soft wool and sensible silk, accessorized by a touch of vermillion at the neck, an eighteen-inch gold chain and a slim tennis bracelet at her wrist to feminize the power image. Her voice was soft and brittle, the aural counterpart of a perfect crème brulée. She shied easily, like a racehorse, and she was good-looking in a horsey way too, upper-class and waspy, though her eyes were too dark and velvety for the Anglo-Saxon part.

She invited us to sit down, asked if we'd like coffee.

"Cream and sugar," said the Frog.

"Of course," said Silver, frowning. She was a cross between a leftover child and a *Vogue* model, I decided. Wistful and imperious, commanding and apologetic—"I hope it's not too cold," she said when the coffee was brought in—semi-detached and apparently committed, Silver was as oxymoronic as a soft cookie with a hard center: the poor little rich girl on whose braceleted wrist, like a falconer's strap, rested the control of Harrier.

Her nails drummed a constant tattoo on the edge of the desk. She listened to Gernreich without appearing to hear him, but every now and then she deflated his bombast with a pointed question. Occasionally she looked at me with an appraising glance, as if measuring me for draperies. Sometimes, from nowhere, a smile landed on her face to remain only a few seconds before taking off again. "Nobody likes changing horses in midstream," she said suddenly. "The paperwork . . . and the delays."

The meeting lasted twenty minutes. She stood up abruptly and waved us to the door. "Nice meeting you," she said. "Good luck."

Another crisp virgilian guide escorted us back the way we'd come, out through the labyrinth, past the pit where the receptionist sat, ignoring us with her back. Outside the glass doors, the Frog and I shook hands. Silver had approved me, as he'd predicted. We were partners now, officially.

Research

Halloween to Thanksgiving to Christmas to New Year's. In the Beginning was research: all aspects of wine and wine-making from the days of Noah and Bacchus to the vineyards of Napa and Sonoma. The Frog urged me to go to California and see for myself, as he'd done during the gestation of the outline, touring the wine country where the grapes of *Vines* were stored. But I couldn't afford such high-flown research yet. I hadn't been paid and wasn't sure when I would be or even, when the time came, how much I'd get. Harrier had distributed the advance due on signing months earlier, when Gernreich was working with his former collaborator, and the next payment wasn't due until acceptance of the completed manuscript. As inventor and onlie begetter of Knightsbridge, the Frog was keeping his full share of the initial advance (it was his baby, after all, that had been bought by Harrier), and this meant that whatever money I'd receive during the writing of the book would have to be recouped from the original writer. Malady was negotiating on my behalf, but meanwhile I had to keep my research expenses down.

No flights to California; I stayed close to home, buying only those books I thought essential, and mainly relying on our local library (an excellent one, in fact): I consulted *The Reader's Guide to Periodical Literature,* recently transferred to microfilm, and read everything by Robert M. Parker, Jr. I invested in my own copy of *What Every Investor Needs to Know about Wines,* which I ordered by mail from Dow-Jones Irwin. I took out a subscription to *The Wine Advocate* and wrote to the Food & Wine Society in London asking for any information they could send me. I discovered the little-known *Wine-Growers Monthly* and something called

Wine & Health, which turned out to be the oenophobic ravings of a Reverend J. Fullerton Blight, who advocated a return to Prohibition. I read Alexis Lichine, André Simon, Alexis Bespaloff and Frank J. Prial. All the reading and exploring exhilarated me; I was back in my element, a journalist again as when I'd worked on *The Care and Feeding,* doing the research, getting the facts, discovering what there was to learn and feeling my way into a new field of knowledge. I spent hours in liquor stores, particularly those that specialized in wines. The racks became my other library, though not a lending one. I explored the shelves with eyes and hand, studying labels, trying to memorize the names of producers and shippers, checking the vintages against my vintage guide and trying to guess the price of a bottle before I picked it up and looked. Sometimes I fell into a sublime form of supermarket trance, wandering through the rows. Mouton Rothschild, the Montrose 1970, a Romanée-Conti I drank . . .

. . . in London, in the sixties, dining on Charlotte Street with an elderly gent who offered it in foretaste to whatever I might later return as cordial. I think his name was Norman, though it might have been Cromwell. In my mouth, it expanded. Queen of Burgundies, he called it; a seven-year-old wonder then, evolving through its ages as I drank, from youth to ripeness—to a maturity so rich, complex, so filled with innuendo that as I drank I longed for it; and in the aftertaste I felt . . .

Nostalgie de la bouteille.

Chambertin, Pommard, Margaux; Bordeaux and Burgundies, *exceptionnels* and *hors.* In fantasy I drank the best, the reds mainly, though an occasional Graves or Haut Brion would do. But not Sauternes and not Champagne.

It was a sad irony that I'd never developed a taste for it. The bubblies always left me flat. I did the research, gathered data, studied hard, but had no insights. The meaning evaded me. Like a biographer who feels no sympathy for her subject, I had the facts but lacked the love.

The Frog gave me Xeroxes of his clippings and notes. To these I added my own and my files were growing, visibly spreading over the room.

"Just do it, Mom," Becky kept urging me. "Get into it." She was impatient of process and preliminaries; at sixteen, she favored metamorphosis over other methods of growth or development. Becky could wake up in the morning and find she'd turned into a numismatist, or a sex fiend or a baseball addict. If Mom was going to turn into a best-selling author, why not overnight?

Because I was into reading. I was still taking notes, clipping articles, making Xeroxes. Also, I was reading popular fiction. I read them all: the Briskins and Bobbins, the Collins and Crowns, sleazy and soapy. Once I started I couldn't stop. Joellen was right, they were popcorn, insubstantial but filling, leaving no room or desire for more solid fare.

"Which of you bitches is my mother?"—*Lace*. The awfulness of it sent shivers down my spine. Tasteless, tacky, vulgar—irresistible. The characters were paper cutouts, collages, put together with the glue of plot. Glue, goo, that icky, sticky goo—and the ickiness made it that much more fun to wallow in.

The Sheldons, the Sidneys, the Harolds, the Irvings: men could do it just as well as women. Less frills and lace maybe, but just as addictive, just as unreadable, unputdownable. The Jameses, the Cliffords, the Roberts, the Johns: they rammed and zapped and thrust and fucked and took me, unresisting, along the torrents of their prose, through the terrible things that happen to terrible people: their scandals and avarice, murders and rapes; the coveting of neighbors' possessions and neighbors' wives; the dishonoring of father and mother; the taking of names (and verbs and pronouns) in vain; the graven idols; the bearing of false witness; the sins of pride, covetousness, lust, anger, envy, sloth: all of the deadly seven except for gluttony.

> Forthreaching to the fruit, she pluckt, she et,
> Earth felt the wound, and Nature from her seat . . .

(what I was reading was forbidden fruit, poisonous, delectable)

> Gave signs that all was lost . . .

(though never here, in books like these: if paradise seemed lost awhile, it would turn out only to have been mislaid and would be found again before the novel's end in paradise regained.)

Wonderful stuff. My thoughts learned to skip like a flat stone over water. I had become one with my reader. Tell me what a person reads and I'll tell you what she writes. I was ready to begin.

IV

WHAT IS
A COMMERCIAL
NOVEL?

Commercial fiction is to fiction what a commercial holiday is to a holiday, says V. It's nearly the same thing, in other words, and many people can't tell the difference between them. It lies in the significance.

Valentine's Day, I handed in the first 280 pages, close to the water mark left by my predecessor. It covered most of Section I, taking Fleur up to the time of her first period.

The Frog hadn't seen any of it until then. He'd thought it best for me to be alone with *Vines* at the beginning, in something like a confinement or lying-in, to help me come to think of it as my own baby. He'd wait, he said, until I came to a natural stopping point, whenever I wanted him to take a look. Any problems along the way though, he was there to help. "Night or day. Call when you need me." He carried a beeper and, true to his word, returned my calls like a doctor in emergency.

When I was ready to show him the typescript, I delivered it by hand, not trusting the mails. "You should get a word processor," he said. "When I'm rich," I told him, though I knew that if I were I wouldn't.

"If you had one, we could work by modem."

Modem? What could that be, I wondered, except a processed form of demon? "Certainly not," I said and, placing the precious bundle in his arms, I deadheaded home, light and empty, my fate in his hands.

Next morning he called and I drove back in. We sat at the long kitchen table, chocolate babka set between us, his new cappuccino-maker frothing on the counter as if plugged in to a rabies attack. The tone was fine, he said, he liked the writing, but the last sixty pages would have to be cut because of a minor character who'd taken over the narrative and was threatening to run away with the book.

She'd entered the novel by means of a passing reference in the outline to a cleaning lady, had taken on the name Celestine and had weaseled her way through the pages of *Vines* for nearly three chapters, holding Philippe captive as she narrated the story of her life, wheezing and coughing during her large bursts of dialog. She'd been asthmatic since childhood; she was raped by her step-father and ran away from home at the age of thirteen to join the circus. She became engaged to the lion tamer, "a perverted man," as she later described him, who'd been mauled by a lioness and deprived of his manhood when he was attempting to commit a bestial act with one of her cubs. After this, Celestine left the circus

and became a stripper, but her attacks of coughing left the customers cold. She was fired. Things went from bad to worse: "My
life, *monsieur,* has been due to unfortunate circumstances."

"Don't worry about it," said the Frog after he'd X'd the pages.
"These things happen. It's what you'd expect, starting out. A lot
of characters will be competing for the spotlight, but you got to
hold them back. Though you got to give them some rein too,
enough to see what they're like, see if you can use them. But this is
Fleur's book, remember. A lion-tamer screwing a cub we don't
need."

"Of course not." I flushed, remembering what I'd accused him
of when I first read the outline.

"And we don't need child abuse either. But you can't always
tell. Sometimes a character crops up who's dynamite for the story.
You got to give these people a chance to breathe if they want to,
but be ready to strike them."

Character, plot, narrative: all novels, commercial or otherwise,
are composed of the same ingredients. Also, dialog, theme, setting,
and the potpourri known as "techniques": transitions and flash-
backs, metaphors, symbolism, and all the devices, artificial and otherwise ("prostheses and dildos," V calls them) that authors depend
on to further the action. Outwardly, they're very much the same.
In fact, the surface layer of novel type 1 and novel type 2 is so similar that passages from one could be grafted onto the other without
danger of rejection.

And there's nothing about the size or weight of the books that
tells them apart. Though commercial novels tend to be long (a
bargain in paperback at a penny a page), the same is true of *Ulysses,*
Moby Dick and *War and Peace,* not to mention *Remembrance of*
Things Past in all its volumes.

The actual process of writing doesn't vary much from one

writer to another, either. Tolstoy or the author of *Tarzan*, it's the same rush of adrenalin, the sustained high in an ecstasy of words, no matter if it issues as Art or babble. ("That's not particular to writers," V insists. She decided to give a course on The Commercial Novel when I began writing *Vines*. "The cabbie who dreams up a new way to rig his meter feels the same way. It's a sense of omnipotence, the by-product of invention. "Satan's revenge," she calls it, on the model of Montezuma's.)

A commercial novel is a novel that issues at a premature stage of development. It reads like an early draft of the real thing. Adjectives and adverbs abound, dead images proliferate . . .

"An unweeded garden, possessed by nature merely, not yet art," V says. "Extended metaphors should be nipped in the bud."

The clichés have been left in (though perhaps intentionally, to reassure the reader with a sense of familiarity and make her feel at home in the book); characters retain bizarre parts of the anatomy, like pits of stomachs or bottoms of hearts, and all their organs function in peculiar ways. Brains "curdle," skin "crawls," blood "boils"; hearts "melt" and wombs "rejoice." Minds "lurch" or "shrink" in horror and souls, if they exist, are often pregnant. (As an example, take the Number 1 best-seller at the time: "Her body and face were blazing hot, her reason decimated by great, turbulent emotions. Yet she was surging with helpless despair" (*Everything and More*). Later in the book, "Her facetiousness rang . . . in the afternoon shadows.") Fear is often deep-seated, like an armchair; quivering thighs give the lie to their firmness; the quality of hope is described as a jack-in-the-box, springing up to land a blow to eyes or breast.

All novels have something of this in them, at least at the beginning. The bizarreries, lapses, the terrible passages of over-writing or simple gibberish; the impossible, ridiculous, and excruciating: the embarrassments of a rough draft.

"Revise that," V says. "Cut it out! You can't write purple prose without going purple. Take it away!"

"All of it?"

"Most of it. 'Quivering thighs give the lie . . . ' That's hideous. You think Montaigne let it all come out like toothpaste? Revise and shine! Polish those passages. There's no such thing as a natural writer except for a lazy one. Any fool can write; a writer rewrites. Rewriting is what separates the pros from the con artists."

She's right, of course. The most difficult job in writing is rewriting. It calls for a ruthlessness and strength of will unknown to any other human endeavor except for the cleaning-out of closets, the discarding of what you don't really need or haven't worn, no matter how beautiful, how expensive or by how many sentimental strings you're attached to it. To throw out an otherwise perfect passage simply because it doesn't fit is the highest form of self-denial.

A novel begins in chaos and proceeds to order. From feeling to form; write drunk; revise sober.

✍   ✍   ✍

I returned to the typewriter and made the necessary revisions. I excised Celestine, removed all traces of her and picked up the narrative from before she'd existed. In early March I was accepted at an artists' colony in the northern woods, among quaking aspen and silver birch with a view of the bald purple mountain. There, freed of responsibility, of household, telephone, feeding the cat and preparing the dinner, I could write again the way I had before I married. I let the words come, the sentences flow, and I was already babbling in the early morning before the birds came into song.

"Being so caught up, so mastered . . ." When I married, inheriting the twins and fifteen months later becoming a mother myself, I was caught up in obligations, hours to keep. I worked like a bank clerk, nine to five, and eventually my muse took off. But at the colony I could escape, into or from myself; I sloughed off the layers of domesticity and wrote like a fiend.

"I like having my family around when I'm working," Norman Mailer said to me after dinner one evening in Provincetown, decades ago.

"That's because you don't have to think about the sugar," I told him.

"What sugar?"

His wife understood. The sugar that someone has to remember to buy. Or the milk, or dinner. The laundry that has to be done, things brought to the cleaners, the cat to the vet and the car for inspection. She's an artist herself (or actress or journalist). Doesn't matter; being a wife is a service occupation.

Before I married, the problem was sex, not groceries. Or maybe it was identity, not sex. Either way, I had to act out the part of girl/woman to reassure myself that I was not merely a writer but a sex object as well. It was hard to be both in the same place and time. Being a woman was not simply a matter of gender then; it was more of an impersonation. I did it in London: platinum blonde, low-cleavaged, until I couldn't stand it anymore and I'd go off to the country to write undisturbed and obsessively, leaving behind all distinguishing marks of sex, age or other forms of social identity, becoming simply a funnel for the words to rush through, coursing to the end of a novel in the space of a few weeks. Then I'd return to the city and become a girl again, waking in time to drown my hangover in the pub before lunch, going on through the evening, into the night, taking in and putting out until I fell into dreamless sleep, to wake when a pounding in my head sounded the bugle that it was time to rise. A few weeks or months of that and I was ready to take off again, leaving the city when a sense of acute discomfort, similar to gas pains, told me it was time to flush. I was like a cistern, the way I worked: words and images filling up slowly in the unnoticed regions of my debauch until the persistent pain alerted me, and I'd bolt to the country to let it all out in a woosh!

At the colony I could work again in that maniacal way. Satan's revenge: the words streamed out, leaping like fish. I averaged more than a hundred pages a week, and when I returned home after five weeks, I had a total of 776 pages (including the section I'd written before): the first draft, completed.

✍ ✍ ✍

PACE is crucial, the single most important element in a commercial novel. The popcorn factor, without which the book stands no chance of being published, much less read. The pace must be kept fast, breathless if not breakneck: at no point may the reader get bored, even for an instant, or stop to question, or to wonder. Suspension of disbelief depends on giving her no time to think. Accelerate! Keep those pages turning. Speed absolves inconsistencies of style, the spelling errors, grammatical mistakes, misuse of words or malapropisms, the missing foundations of underlying structure—repetitions and replays, the omission of scenes. "I must have missed something awhile back," the reader tells herself, but it doesn't matter, she keeps on going.

A publisher told me that one of his blockbusters had come out, was in the stores and already on the best-seller list when he happened to pick it up and noticed that a character who'd been killed off early in the book reappeared on page 362 and continued to take part in the narrative as if nothing was amiss until he died again, in a particularly affecting scene fifty pages later. The problem had been caused by grafting two versions of the novel onto each other without removing the overlap, but no one among all the readers, not even in the publishing house, had caught it. Pace is everything.

"Except for character," says V. "Character is something too."

✍   ✍   ✍

From the colony's pay phone near the dining room I spoke to the Frog at least twice a week. I looked forward to these calls and came away from them exhilarated. I reported on the work I was doing; every ten days or so I sent him a Xerox of my new chapters. He praised me, encouraged me, told me I was everything he'd hoped for, and more. I believed him. I grew very fond of the Frog during my retreat; more than that, I came to rely on him. We were in this together, partners in name, father and mother to the same offspring, bound by *Vines,* our fortunes linked. Sometimes I dreamed about him, his muddy eyes speckled with green, a tender look on his face. He held me by his soft pads like a midwife toad and I woke feeling aroused.

Analysts call this "transference"—using a stand-in when the regular actor doesn't show up. Analysts expect to be the ones chosen for the leading role—usually Father, occasionally Husband. But I didn't think of the Frog as either. He was too small, not as good-looking or sexy. (My father's a charmer and Arthur is a knockout.) My feelings for the Frog were tender and protective, the way you feel about a tooth or breast.

I didn't breathe a word of how I felt to anyone. No one would have believed me in any case. Malady would be merely confused, Becky (to whom I'd described him physically) would make a rude noise of some kind, Arthur would smile the way he does when I refer to country music or when an auto mechanic tries to give him the details of what's wrong with the transmission, and V would dismiss my remark as a failed attempt at satire. Thinking of the Frog as part of myself would have struck her as ludicrous; she would have demanded to know which part; and if I then confessed that I saw the two of us as somehow fused, or siamesed, through our joint labor, she would have told me to throw out the sentence like a pair of wet socks.

Like a teenager, I kept it to myself. But as soon as I came home from the colony I called the Frog and made a date for the following day. I washed my hair that night and next morning went through five changes of clothing before I was dressed. But for all that, nothing changed. We met in the Village, he was small and round, his eyes still muddy, no hint of green.

We took the typescript to be Xeroxed, a copy for Harrier, another for Malady, each of us paying half the cost, and afterwards we went to lunch at a small French Provincial restaurant, brick walls, fresh flowers on the table. When he ordered champagne to celebrate, I made no objection, and after the first few glasses was surprised to find it almost pleasurable. Either my taste was changing or I'd never before understood that the beverage was intended for drinking in the early part of the day.

"To us," he said again.

"To us," I repeated.

"I'm proud of you, Kate. You did a fantastic job."

"Fantastic." I remembered his soft pads and thought of hugging him. Then I thought better of it; I would reserve my impulses for times when he wasn't actually present.

"Terrific speed. You made it to the finish in no time at all. Speeds Kate, what a name for a horse."

"Not really." I meant it wasn't the finish line yet, only the first draft. The final version was due in about ten weeks, and before that it would have to be edited, revised and possibly rewritten.

"When it's accepted, I'll take you to Lutèce."

"All you can eat for a thousand dollars?"

"That's the place."

When the check came we split it, though he pocketed the receipt for the full amount. "Tax," he explained. "Business expenses." Since I hadn't been paid yet, I wouldn't need deductions, he pointed out, though in his bracket, it meant he'd be getting at least a third off. He walked me to my car and told me to relax for the next few days, forget about the book, do anything I wanted to do. I'd more than earned it, he said. In any case, it would take weeks to hear back from Harrier, and though I might want to work on his suggestions before then, the notes and comments he'd made along the way, he'd wait to send them to me until after my little vacation.

I didn't know what to do with it. I spent a day with Becky, morning to night, my nerves raw at the end of it. It wasn't her fault; I was suffering from a condition known as re-entry, its symptoms familiar to fellows of artists' colonies or prisoners or nuns when they come out into the real world. I wasn't used to being with someone else for such long periods, and though I loved Becky, cherished and adored her, it was hard work to keep up with her after my spell in the secluded woods. With Arthur I didn't have the problem. He was rarely around, and when he was, he was working. My symptoms dissipated after a few days, but Arthur remained in his study, devoting himself to the syntax of ancient Greek. We had little to say to each other now in any case; our worlds had become so different that it was nearly impossible to translate between them.

V was leaving for California. She'd written a play called *The Health Club*, a comedy about dying, and a producer was interested in discussing its potentials as a musical, aerobic song and dance and clean nudity in the steam room virtually assuring its release under a PG rating.

I went to the airport to see her off, ten in the morning, La Guardia, but as soon as I caught sight of her across the lobby, I wanted to escape before she noticed me. She was looking unusually Harry, but in a rumpled way, her hair sliding into the collar of her coat like wet seaweed. Overweight, badly dressed, her coat several sizes too small, wearing patent leather loafers in a shade of bright lavender—she saw me and waved. I turned away as if looking for someone behind me; then turned back and, smiling like a villain, walked towards her quickly, aware of the people watching us, of their curiosity or contempt as they looked at her, trying to figure out if it was a man or a woman, and then at me, wondering what we did together. When I came up to her she reached for my hand. "Sorry," she said. I didn't know why she was apologizing, but I felt the people staring and I pulled her close to me and kissed her on the mouth.

And then regretted it, and then felt ashamed. We had breakfast together and, when the flight was called, I walked her to the departure gate. I watched her go through the metal detector and down the long corridor, making her way between departures and arrivals, a person somewhere between male and female. Could this be a metaphor, I wondered? Is everything? A metaphor for what?

The next time I saw V—but I'm getting ahead of myself again. We are trying to answer a question here. We're aiming for a definition. What is a commercial novel? We want the FACTS.

✍ ✍ ✍

Fact in fiction, fact as fiction—readers of the purple sages are looking for knowledge or at least information when they read. "What's the book about?" they want to know. Hollywood or

Hawaii, dress designing, wine-making, the papacy, or military life in the Middle Ages—the "about" part of a novel is what captures the reader. Dickens was a master at this, Balzac too: the detailed workings of the French railway system or the inside story of the Revolution. The reader wants to find out, to become informed about something without having to go through the actual work of looking it up or doing research. To know more than the neighbors and to know it better. The lure of popular fiction isn't sex, as Joellen's "some people" might think, it's Finding Out.

CHARACTER is the hook that pulls the reader into the story. ("Which of you bitches is my mother?") The Heroine is the reader's other, fantasized self—richer, more attractive, successful, more talented—who must suffer for the advantages she has. (The world's most beautiful woman, unable to find love. The heiress with a lingering illness, the movie star with a drinking problem.) Since the reader envies her, the heroine must be flawed in a way that allows the reader to feel superior (to a woman obviously better than herself), and to take pity on her.

Pity is an acceptable and self-gratifying form of revenge. Whatever there is in the world of happiness, beauty, fame or wealth, the reader feels, exists only in limited quantities, and whatever portion of it has been dished out to someone else (the heroine) means there's less left for me. Feeling sorry for the heroine mitigates the reader's envy and allows her (the reader) to identify.

The Hero must be worthy of her (the heroine, the reader). He's a simple figure usually: simply perfect. What every woman deserves: an ardent lover (but deeply understanding), brilliant and successful (though supportive of her), protective but never interfering, mature and boyish, both handsome and faithful. Formed of such stuff as dreams are made on, he's something else and out of this world. Cream for the reader.

Villains are purely evil, friends are true (unless they're rivals) and lovers are either heroes or antiheroes, depending on whether they turn out to be The Man She Marries or The Other Kind.

SEX comes in two forms: with Him and with Others (also called Foreigners). With Him it's wonderful, vague and synesthetic: pounding hoofbeats, surging tides, exploding colors, smell of lilacs, taste of love. (A woman who was once the mistress of Orson Welles reported that his skin tasted of honey and almonds.) It's hugely cinematic, music swelling to crescendo, fireworks and lightning storm, fruit ripening, blossoms bursting in fast forward, the great wave rising and silver dawn beyond the tide. With a Foreigner it's graphic: the tools laid out, the nuts and bolts described. It's real, it's porn. A user's guide.

Sex and LOVE are handled like different genres. Sex is porn and love Romance, each with its rules and specifications. When I was writing porn, even though it was for "straight" rather than "special-interest" magazines (the latter are those devoted to a particular sexual activity, like buggery or bondage, or to an anatomical predilection, like huge breasts or hairy mounds), I learned to follow certain conventions. Within each story there was a formula: a single line of development, action proceeding from simple to complex, but orgasm always achieved in the same manner. To illustrate: if Roxanne gives head in the first incident, she must continue to do so throughout the story, though numbers may vary and sizes increase. If Joy is caught in a golden shower after the prom, she will be doused ever after; and if Gloria and Angela fondle each other's breasts in incident 1, they must fondle more fondly as the pages turn.

Porn, like Romance, meets the reader's expectations, no more and no less. Porn can be difficult, but Romance is impossible. I'd discovered that in England, after my first novel was published and the editor of a well-paying woman's mag asked me to write for them. She gave me a list of fourteen specifications for their stories, including the acceptable age difference between hero and heroine (not more than a few years, and he had to be older), the amount of alcohol they were allotted (very little) and cigarettes (none), their social, ethnic and religious backgrounds (no mixing), and an absolute proscription on internal monolog, dreams, and Freudian references. Virginity was a requirement for all unmarried females, and if they made a living it was not to be mentioned. What about dialog, I asked? (Being American, I thought, might make it hard for my characters to sound convincingly British). Not to worry, she said. "Write in your own language, dear; we'll Anglicize afterwards."

I couldn't do it, of course; I lacked the sincerity. Besides, the characters offended my morality. But two decades later, when Fleur came into existence, heroines were possessed of careers and sexuality. They enjoyed sex and were good at it, even when the Man was a Foreigner.

I took Fleur through several affairs before she married—her initiation, as the Frog had outlined, was with a woman—and brought her to orgasm in each encounter. (The Frog had instructed me never to leave her unsatisfied; even with an inappropriate or disreputable partner, a Foreigner of any description, Fleur was to enforce her inalienable right, the right of every woman, to come.)

But sex is sex and love is love. Though love includes sex, and may even take root in it, they are not equivalent. Love is the whole, sex is the parts. Love is the fruit and the flower and the storm and the pounding waves and horses on the sand. It is extremely difficult to write without embarrassment.

Sex is not as bad, though it can be tedious, in the manner of technical writing, and finding the right terms is sometimes tricky. Vocabulary straddles between the clinical (vagina), the rough (twat) and the circumlocutional (the dense thicket of her fur). There's always the possibility of sounding ludicrous.

Before I became Knightsbridge, I was squeamish, reluctant to write what I couldn't want to read. But afterwards I wrote fearlessly. If I lost heart in attempting a scene of licentious congress or loving embrace, I simply lifted one from a current best-seller (Krantz, Collins, Robbins—usually Krantz), changed the characters' names, what they wore and the place where they did it (a field of sunflowers for a sunlit floor, a speedboat for an antique biplane) and let it ride as my own. I'd become popularity's scribe, daring the improbable, switching roles and genres and changing my colors as I fed off the air, the chameleon's dish.

Characters on Their Own

When V said, "Sorry," I assumed she was echoing my distress at her appearance. But when she returned from California, I realized that what she'd meant was something more complicated. Her disheveled appearance had been part of an overall transformation, Harry rising again from V's cocoon, and I was seeing her at a stage of metamorphosis not yet completed, somewhere between chrysalis and wings. She'd known then that she would see Carole while she was out there, and was apologizing to me for what she suspected would happen.

The next time I saw V she was Harry and in love, sexually charged, as appealing as the first time we'd met, in the bar with Mike. Carole, I learned, was as tall as myself, a journalist. I felt betrayed; I expected V in my life now, not Harry, and by switching character she was changing the perspective—"Sorry"—and forcing me to switch POV (point of view) in mid-paragraph, one of the most elementary blunders in writing fiction.

Is it natural to interpret the behavior of others as if it were directed toward oneself? Is it an occupational disease of writers to cast the people they meet within the novel of their life? Is this megalomania? paranoia? or a common perversity, linked to the storytelling gene and preserved since the dawn of *homo sapiens* as an adaptation that permits the individual to view his life as a novel and enables him to give meaning to his existence beyond replication and death? What if two writers cast each other within their separate novels? Who's who then? Or do we live as in a dream, wherein all the characters are aspects of ourselves? If I left V out of this novel, would she still exist? would I? as whom?

In the airport, about to fly to California to discuss her play with a producer and to enter a new love affair (as a new person?), V was speaking through her own concerns, not mine, though what I heard applied only to me. In a novel, events and characters are controlled by the author. A best friend or lover (or even a cleaning lady) doesn't simply go her own way. She stays within the expectations of the book, or else she's exiled from it, left to disintegrate or to wander in the limbo of lost characters searching for a novel.

"All novels," an editor told me once, "begin with departures or arrivals." He didn't mean airports. He was talking about the point at which action is about to develop. Action toward or from an event, like shipping off to sea as a whaler, or waking to discover you've turned into a cockroach. The story begins immediately before or after something happens to change a life.

When I first met the Frog I was going nowhere, collecting kill fees, my writing unpublished. "You'll make me rich," he promised, offering in return a new beginning. Six months later I'd written the first draft of *Vines* and was transformed. I'd become a part of his invention, the -bridge into a new existence.

As Jacqueline, coupling with the Frog's imagination and spawning nearly 800 pages of prose, I'd been brought to life again. Writing under an assumed name, animated by my creator (like Winnie the Pooh, who lived "Under the Name of Saunders"), no longer accountable for what I wrote, freed from doubts, standards and ego, I let the sentences come, corks pop, champagne bubble and sex explode.

It was exhilarating, a new departure more than twenty years after first setting out; sailing forth again after years in drydock, waking to write and writing in my dreams: this was living. I didn't want to stop.

But the Frog hadn't finished going over the manuscript yet. A few days after I was back from the Colony, I began to get bored, then restless, finally frantic. I wanted to get to work on the revisions, start a new draft. I needed my daily fix of Knightsbridge. But whenever I called, he said to give him a few more days.

The days dragged to weeks. Becky was in the final throes of her dying youth (as she called it), graduation less than two months away and senescence winking from the other side of high school as she seized the day and the nights with her comings and goings, turning the front door into a revolving one with all her merry-go-round friends, their music blaring, their theme song endlessly repeating: "I / Wanna rock-an-roll all ni-ight / And party ev-er-y day." It was hideous. I needed *Vines* to cling to for life and sanity.

The Frog was still not ready. He had other projects to set in motion. Besides, he said, there was no point giving me his comments until we'd heard what Harrier had to say. He'd wait until then. Malady said she'd wait too. It was clear that neither of them wanted to venture on what they now regarded as Harrier's property. It was up to the editor at this point, and though Winnie Silver had chosen to honor us by selecting the Knightsbridge as one of the handful of books she edited each year, the honor was becoming an increasingly empty one. She was inundated by other work, mainly administrative, and couldn't get around to it, but, because she was still intending to, she was unwilling to assign the job to someone else.

Deadline was approaching, only three weeks away. The Frog was licking cream off his fingers at the Riviera. He'd rented a castle in Ireland for the summer, he said. Good for the kids, they could climb up the ruins.

What about *Vines*? I asked him. What about the deadline?

"Deadlines don't matter." The shortcake was stale, he decided; maybe he should try the Mississippi mud.

"Don't matter?" I repeated. "Then why . . . ?"

"You got to act like you're going for it, if you're the author, but publishers don't really expect a book to come in on time. A deadline's just something they have to put in a contract. I've already asked Malady to get us the next installment of the advance."

"But that's not due until acceptance of the completed manuscript," I reminded him.

"So what? It's nearly July 1, time for them to pay up."

The logic wasn't absolutely transparent to me. In an effort to clear things up, I asked when we'd be having our lunch at Lutèce.

"Don't worry, we'll do it—we'll go Dutch."

Dutch? Lutèce? What I'd received so far for my work on *Vines* had gone into kitchen windows, a few groceries and Becky's graduation present, a trip across America.

"After I'm back," he added. "We'll have the check by then. Where will you be spending the summer?"

"Home," I said bitterly, "working on *Vines.*"

"There's a phone in the castle," he said, "and another in the ruins. You can always reach me."

"Thanks." To show my contempt, I offered to pay for his food and my coffee; he handed me the check.

The deadline passed and we still had no editor. Becky was on her cross-country trip, the Frog in Ireland and Arthur in Greece, attending a conference. I couldn't have gone along even if he'd asked me (he hadn't), or if we'd had the money; I had to be standing by for the return of *Vines.*

I'd made my departure but now I was stuck, waiting at home in flypaper summer. Departures are fine for beginnings and endings, but between them is the tedium of the transit lodge, where nothing really happens. Or if it does, if something unexpected occurs, it will inevitably seem out of place or unbelievable. In London in the sixties a waitress at the old Lyons Corner House on Picadilly

Circus said to me: "Sometimes I feel that I have measured out my life in coffee spoons."

The mind boggles. How could someone *really* say that? They also serve who only stand and wait.

It was late July before Winnie Silver called in an outside editor, Bianca Lichtgrau, whose reputation befitted her name as the *eminence grise* of popular fiction, now Harrier's white hope. Over the years, Bianca had coached dozens of novels into best-sellerdom, relying on an uncanny and nearly infallible instinct for sensing the reader's feelings as though they were her own. She knew what would offend and what would titillate; she could feel when the time was right for a character to die or make love or recover from illness. (Fleur was scheduled to lose her virginity on the day Robert Kennedy was assassinated, but Bianca knew her readers would disapprove: "Too heartless." It didn't matter that Camus' hero makes love to a woman immediately after his mother's funeral, or that the wife of Bath sallies from graveyard to bed. Fleur belonged to her readers, and though she could lie in bed with the young man, exchanging chaste embraces after the terrible event, she was made to observe a period of mourning before penetration could take place.)

Bianca worked wonders. She was as brilliant in her way as the Frog in his; through her Knightsbridge became a trinity. She edited the manuscript in less than a month, covering each of the pages with blue paper flags containing queries, comments, suggestions. She also asked for some major revisions. Whatever she asked for, I did. The Frog had mailed his notes to her from the castle in Ireland and she scrupulously forwarded them to me without comment, except for small penciled checks here and there, allowing me the illusion of free choice while at the same time telling me what to do.

When he returned around Labor Day, he asked if his suggestions had been helpful. I told him yes, and that was that. He didn't ask if I was incorporating any of them; he seemed to sense that it was time for him to retreat from *Vines* a while. The novel was in Bianca's custody now, and he moved with great delicacy, soft pads on Bianca's turf.

It was late fall again before the final draft was in. Then came copy-editing and layout, and it was midwinter before the novel was finally at the printer's. By this time others had made their departures too.

V was spending most of her available time in California, working on the play or playing with Carole. My old friend Mike was in Africa on what he called a sabbatical. Though he was not employed by an academic institution—or by anyone else—he'd decided to broaden his field of expertise by taking a few months' leave from people and spending it in the company of other types of animals instead. He was particularly anxious to live among the elephants, for whom he'd conceived an almost intolerable longing and whose days he knew to be numbered. He suspected them of being not only larger and more attractive than humans, but more interesting as well.

The characters were changing, running away with their own concerns, recasting themselves beyond my context. Mainly, they were thinning out.

Becky had started college in September, and though she'd come home every weekend for the first five of the semester, seeking refuge from the extraterrestrials who she claimed taught her classes or attended them, she'd eventually become habituated to her new planet and didn't want to leave. She was held there by magnetism, she explained, whose name turned out to be Bo (I'd thought it was *beau* until I saw it written) and he was big, blond and shaggy like her father. He was an old man too, she told me, he'd been drinking (legally) for more than two years. But when I told her to bring him along, she found other reasons not to come: ball games, her studies, a pajama party in the dorm—too many reasons. Partly, I suspected, she was staying away because of her fear of me, now that I was alone.

Arthur had moved out when he returned from Greece, saying that I'd lost my soul or in any case misplaced it. He claimed I wasn't the woman he'd married, that I'd become the Frog's creation, no longer his.

How could I argue? If someone invents you as part of his story, there's not much you can do to change it. History or hers, who you think you are is not the same as who you're taken for. I was bitter, of course; more than that, I was devastated. Who was there for me to turn into? V had retreated into the persona she'd devised before I married, but I was the mother of a nearly grown child and had lost my dramatic license.

Becky was now close to the age I'd been when I'd fallen in love with Arthur, with Arthur and his nights: in the Age of Romance. We'd waged our marriage as others do, in uneasy alliance but allies just the same, until my pact with the Frog placed us in opposing camps.

It was too late to turn back, or to transform myself into someone I might have become if I'd lived my life differently (like V or Harry), aspiring neither to God nor starlet but content to dwell in my own reflections. I'd made my pact thinking it would help me write again, not realizing that you cannot give your soul and keep it too, or return the apple after you've taken a bite.

Whenever she called, Becky tried to reassure me. She wanted me to know she was being supportive. She'd say things like, "You could still get a man if you tried, Mom. Hang out in bars."

I thanked her, hung up, and burst into tears.

Digression: On Love

1.

I was dreaming about my mother again. When I started on the Knightsbridge, my mother had been dead three years. Her death freed me in many ways, though I couldn't stop thinking about her. After she died I dreamed about her every night for more than a year. The dreams were always the same: she came back from the dead; I was terrified at seeing her because it invalidated everything I knew to be true about the universe. "You can't be real," I'd tell her. "You can't be here."

"Touch me," she'd say. She was warm and alive.

Every night I resurrected her in dreams. I couldn't bear to think she hadn't loved me enough.

In my dreams now she looked like Arthur.

2.

"Love," said the PR man for Nabisco, at the time I was writing my book on food, "is two hang-ups meeting."

I'd come to pick him up in his office before the interview he'd promised over lunch. He pointed to the couch along the wall: "We can eat right here," he said, and gave me a lascivious wink. Then he took me to The Four Seasons, where he had a telephone brought to the table.

He spoke to his clients during our meal, answering my questions between the calls. "We sell all our products through love," he told me. "A direct pitch for the heart."

3.

"Love was a breakfast cereal once," I said to Becky recently. She went on eating, unimpressed. What difference did it make? On the shelves of supermarkets you find Life and Total Fitness and More. If the cereal box says Real, that doesn't mean anything, it's just a name. Her generation doesn't confuse words with truth; it's a form of innocence that's taken over since the end of satire. When the American vice-president thinks Latin is the language spoken in Latin America (and allows this opinion to be quoted by reporters), irony is no longer possible. We're left with the ridiculous, and it isn't funny.

4.

I'm writing this now, looking back on the events through time and distance, distortions of the telescope, uncertainties of observation. "The act of observing alters that which is observed." I don't remember when or where I first read the quote, and maybe it's a paraphrase, but it's stayed with me since. Heisenberg's principle. Uncertainty: we can't know what we think we know. What we've understood may be only another aspect of ourselves.

What I observe exists only as it is observed by me. The book I write may not be the book you read. Is beauty in the I of the beholder? Is there no truth in fiction? On the contrary; more here than elsewhere.

Better here than Philadelphia. What's to come is still unsure. (Love's a stuff will not endure.)

5.

For most of my life I maintained a double standard, not because I was committed to it in an intellectual sense, or even because I approved of it particularly. It just came naturally to me. What's good for the goose is good for the goose. When I was younger, it didn't occur to me to be jealous. If a man could have me and instead chose someone else, he was obviously deficient and not worth my attention. After I married, I went on having affairs, but I didn't want *him* to. I was free, but I expected him to be mine.

Without being aware of it, I'd attached myself to him like a barnacle to a rock, and I didn't know how to be free without hanging on.

Digression: On Money

When Harrier's next check came in, Malady took me to lunch at La Cocotte. Harrier's computers run in cycles, like certain diseases carried in the blood and activated by viruses at vaguely predictable intervals. Checks came in with the seasons, Fall and Winter, Spring—but not the Summer. The Frog had wanted Harrier to pay the second part of the advance at the time of the deadline, arguing that "we" had done our job, and that since they'd been the ones holding us up, they had a moral, if not legal, obligation to pay for what might otherwise have been completed. I doubted that *Vines* would have made the deadline in any case, since the revised draft had taken nearly as long as the original, but Harrier had shown its good faith, agreeing to pay half the amount due on completion.

That was in summer, while the computers were dormant. The request was processed in fall, and by the time the good faith shown in New York City had been manifested by their computers in Wisconsin, Alaska or Vladivostock, it was winter. Just before Christmas, Malady received the first installment of $20,000, split the amount into its two Knightsbridge halves, skimmed off her commission of ten percent and sent us each a check for $9,000. When the second check from Harrier arrived three weeks later, she sent me another $9,000 and invited me to lunch.

She's got good instincts; she knew something was wrong. When I told her about Arthur, she nodded. "Success drives them out," she said. It had happened in her own family.

That wasn't the reason, I said. Arthur wouldn't have minded if I supported him the rest of his life. "It's because of . . . "

She held up her hand. "Don't let Gernreich know," she warned me. "He wouldn't like it."

"I understand the feeling," I said, but I didn't need the warning. I knew the Frog wanted me strong and problem-proof. He'd told me that at the beginning. If I turned womanly-woeful now, he might look around for someone else to do the next book. Even if *Vines* would turn out a success.

I wanted it to be a success. I wanted to become very rich. I fantasized about money, I pictured scads and piles of it, in numbers usually, the zeroes repeating, interest compounding. Strangely perhaps, I didn't fantasize about actual possessions. Vaguely, I considered getting a new car, but jewels and money were out, yachts and planes impracticable. I might travel, though, do what Mike did, live among the elephants awhile, maybe find material for a novel of my own. Or go down the Amazon—I remembered wanting to do that at some point. Or to the Galapagos, watch those great, heavy-lidded seeming-deathless creatures move across the sand to drop their eggs; the hatching of the young, the tiny turtles spreading over the beach—they turned to spiders, then to crabs.

I had crabs in England, picked them off and laid them in a row around the seat of the loo when I was lunching at the home of Lady Rose Harlot (or some such name), lady-in-waiting to the Queen. What a lark! Sending crabs to Buckingham Palace. I dined off that (as we used to say) for weeks.

Dining on pheasants, four times in one week, pheasant under glass and white asparagus. Couldn't stand it after the third time, told Noel Coward (or whoever it was) that I'd had a surfeit of game. He took it lightly, thought it was a joke, like a brace of quail.

When I came back, twenty-five-year-old novelist hits town, the editor of *Confidential* asked if I'd write for them. I smiled down at him, poor little man. Sometime around then, I was invited to lunch by Bernie Geis, the publisher, who showed me around the office and introduced me to the resident hermit, a man who spent his day writing poems beside a bonsai tree and who never spoke. I was enchanted by him, a figure straight out of eighteenth-century England, the time when Nonsense ruled the Age of Reason, and ornamental hermits were acquired along with the rest of the chin— or japon—oiserie and remained ensconced in the garden, somewhere beyond the rotunda in sylvan solitude in a folly by the stream. Or Omoo, the Eskimo, brought to London with his family to live in an igloo on the Strand and comment, as a child of nature, on the institutions of the Enlightenment. Self-consciousness raised to the very peak of self-congratulation, of which even the venerable Dr. Swift was guilty, speaking through Gulliver as though he himself were a noble savage. Bernie Geis took me to lunch afterwards, and said he hoped I'd write a book for him. Something with wide appeal, he said he wanted. I'd been thinking of writing a family history then, and I suggested the Jews. Most of them got killed, Bernie reminded me. Not much of a market.

We thrashed around other topics, decided that the national obsession with diet and weight would be good for several million readers at least. The heroine could be a diet doctor, redhead, who has a congressman for a client, maybe a senator or the secretary of state. There could be a scandal attached. I said that sounded nice. He suggested changing my name to Irving, it seemed to do well for authors. First name or last? Didn't matter, he said, Clifford Irving, Irving Wallace—either way was fine, though as a woman, I might want to go with Katherine Irving. I said I'd think about it and excused myself to go to the ladies room. When I came out, someone from the *Ladies' Home Journal* walked up to me and said they'd just acquired the first serial rights to my new book. "In the time it takes to have a pee?" I asked Bernie when I got back to the table. "I told them it was hot," he admitted.

What did it matter then, before the doubts came in? I could talk to anybody about writing anything. Just talk. I knew what I was capable of, I knew that what I wanted more than anything else in the world was to write (sex was a way *into* it, not out of it) and that I had enough to write about and with and for to last me forever. That was Before. The After came slowly, water on rock, but eventually it poured down, destroying what was left of my natural defense.

First time out, I was too cocky, sure of reaching the heights. I spent my time doing what I loved, following my life more than leading it, taken up by the heroine; the narrator, myself. But I'd become bored with her over the years, her predictable situation, the routine of her existence. I'd just written a commercial novel under the name of Knightsbridge because I'd run out of anything to say on my own. Second time around, it was for different stakes. Money, not love. *Vines* was due to be published in May, and I wanted it to be a blockbuster.

V

PRODUCTION

The galleys came back from the printer, looking like no galleys I'd seen before. I was accustomed to those that befitted their name, long and narrow like the sails of dhows, intractable or untackable, sliding out of grasp and underfoot, scampery and slippery, impossible to take out anywhere; slipshod, the print often set at an angle, words running in a diagonal across the margins to the paper's edge; each long sheet a vertical slice of the master sheet, printed from the master plate which represents 64 pages of the actual book. (All books are divisions of 64, including title pages, acknowledgments and dedication, table of contents and the blank filler pages at the beginning and sometimes also at the end. Whenever possible, the actual number of pages is a simple multiple of master plates: 320, 448, 576, 704. That's the cheapest way of setting up a book, though sometimes the text can't be stretched or condensed to fit the Procrustean sheets and it becomes necessary to append another half or quarter master plate: 2 x 64 = 128, plus ⅛ plate (8) = 136 pages.)

Because of the rush to publication, Harrier had decided to dispense with galleys and move directly to page proofs. My proofs of *Vines* arrived in book form, the pages cut and bound between soft covers in a shade of dirty champagne, numbered from 3 to 635 with six unnumbered pages at the beginning and two at the end. A warning was printed on the page preceding the title page: "This advance copy consists of uncorrected manuscript. Material for quotation should be checked against the regular edition." I couldn't see the reason for it—the first sentence seemed self-evident, the second irrelevant (who would think of quoting from an uncorrected proof?)—until Bianca explained that the proofs would be serving a double purpose. Instead of galleys, usually printed up in no more than a handful of copies for use by author(s) and editor(s), what I'd received to work on was both proof and advance reading copy, one in an edition of 3,000, equivalent to the total edition of a first novel and greater than the entire printing of most books of poetry or short stories.

They were intended for "advance readers," she told me, on whose word of mouth Harrier relied to prepare the way for actual publication (tentatively set at a first printing of six to seven hundred thousand copies). These were not the well-known authors who might be persuaded to deliver a quote for use on the dust-jacket or in ads as an endorsement of the book's readability, nor were they reviewers who might be tempted to write about it in newspapers or periodicals (the chances of *Vines* being reviewed anywhere at all were calculated at negative probability); no, the readers' copies were sent instead to a selected vanguard of people

in the trade—though "trade" turned out to be a loose term, referring to anything even marginally involved with the selling or serving of champagne—who would bring the news of the impending
event to clients and customers. Harrier was hoping for approval by
wine and liquor-store owners to pass out copies of *Vines* among
their salespeople, Bianca said. "We're also trying to get books into
the hands of *sommeliers* and bartenders in the top restaurants and
hotels—chains if we can get them, like the Hiltons and Omnis, and
to flight attendants, first and business class mainly. Possibly even
the cruise ships too." Each of the uncorrected proof copies had
cost Harrier approximately $35 to produce—$105,000, I calculated,
to generate what was known as "free" advertising. The published
book would sell for $3.95.

The proofs contained the usual spelling mistakes and a prolifer-
ation of supernumerary punctuation marks, particularly commas. A
few paragraphs were omitted, and a couple had been printed twice.
But the worst printer's error came in the final sentence of the
novel, making it end in nonsense.

Fleur has accomplished her dream; her champagne has taken
the Prix d'Or, the highest accolade in the world of wines, and she
is about to marry Claude, the man she loves, who has been waiting
for nearly twenty years. "She would be forty in another month. In
the bridal salon of Bergman Goodorf, the saleslady asked if she
planned to wear white for her wedding. Fleur smiled. 'I think this
occasion calls for champagne.'"

Instead of "champagne," the word was printed as "change,"
thereby leaving the reader with the unwarranted assumption that
the marriage would not take place after all and depriving her, at
the very last moment, of the happy ending she had every reason to
expect.

Despite the cautionary note at the beginning, I was sure that the misprint would not be recognized as such, since the sentence still made grammatical sense. I phoned the Frog, who said he hadn't had a chance to look at it yet, and told him about the ending. As it stood, it was both flat and misleading; three thousand advance readers would be left with Fleur's unintended spinsterhood.

He took it well. "These things happen," he said with a shrug in his voice. "That's what proofs are for." It would probably be corrected in the published version, and meanwhile I shouldn't worry, since most people wouldn't notice.

Whenever he said things like that, I worried. It gave me an eerie sense of dislocation, as if the whole enterprise were a chimera, Knightsbridge simply a name given to a form of occupational therapy that provided work for multitudes (agents, editors, layout and design people, bookkeepers, booksellers, sales and marketing people, printers, publishers and of course writers) without ever becoming a fact. How could readers *not* notice? What were they reading, if not words?

I called Bianca, who was acting as midwife to another novel, long overdue, and hadn't looked at it either. But she promised to correct the error immediately; she'd see to it that an erratum slip was inserted into each of the advance copies, notifying the reader that *Vines* was meant to end in champagne.

As easy as that, an apology like a band-aid? "Love means never having to say you're sorry"? That's probably the silliest, certainly the most uncompromisingly false sentence ever to be printed, even on a t-shirt. It's from a novel called *Love Story*, which was a tremendous best-seller a few years back, written by a Yale professor with a bird's name who must have taken leave of academia or his senses, going from egghead to airhead. What could he have been thinking of? Apology is defense of love.

Or was it simply a printing error, quoted from uncorrected proofs despite the warning? Maybe the "never" tumbled in from another sentence, landing back to front, its tail lopped off? Reven-ge, as processed by the demon modem? Eros to sore. Love is the mirror of our own illusions. At the beginning, we are One (Madam I'm Adam) in love's palindrome, but love evolves. Two in one leaves none at the end. Between the person I see you as and the one you take me for there will be many errors and omissions, inconsistencies of style, regrettable dialog, lousy transitions and other mistakes of the most obvious kind. The banns of marriage should be published in the form of errata slips.

Vines was going into production. The advertising campaign included a full page ad in *Soap Opera Digest* and a couple of shorter ads in *People*. Books would be delivered to the stores as "dumps"—I pictured wheelbarrows dumped onto the floor, but Bianca assured me this was a technical expression, and *Vines* would be sent to stores with its own display cabinet, a glossy cardboard construction resembling a doll's apartment house, with a four-color riser and base and nine "pockets" (actually cubicles) holding a total of thirty-six copies.

Bianca called when the jacket proof came in and said she was sending me a copy—"unofficially, you understand." I thanked her and promised to keep my opinions to myself. We both knew I had no right to them. My part in *Vines* had officially ended after correcting the proofs. Whatever shares were granted by publisher to author in *Vines* futures belonged exclusively to the Frog, who retained the rights to approval of certain promotion and marketing decisions (including jacket). I told Bianca I wouldn't let him know I'd seen it. He guarded his rights jealously, and in any case had become suspicious of the relationship between Bianca and myself. During the final stages of editing and rewriting, when Bianca and I spoke to each other daily, he'd suspected me of wooing her in some unspecified woman-to-woman way, thereby alienating her affections for him. "She likes you more than me," he'd accused, though he was quick to reassure himself: "But Malady likes *me* better. I make more money for her."

The jacket showed a beautiful blonde with lips parted to receive the spume of champagne newly ejaculated from the bottle. The book's title was embossed in gold script at the top; the author's name appeared further down in smaller print, grape-purple, beneath a caption of the same color announcing, "The fabulous novel of a woman who would stop at nothing to gain her heart's desire."

The back copy was headlined: AMBITION AND LUST AMONG THE VINES . . .

Once in a long while a novel comes along that captures the hearts and minds of readers with its own kind of magic. *VINES* does just that. Breathing with human emotion, it takes us into the glamorous, heady world of champagne. The world of Fleur, a beautiful, lonely woman who dares to set out on a quest few women have attempted.

SHE MUST FIGHT AGAINST MEN AND NATURE . . .

But nothing will stop her. She is prepared to give up everything, including the love of a man she desires, as she struggles to accomplish her dream. Yet she cannot resist the passions in her heart.

In this stunning debut, Jacqueline Knightsbridge plumbs to the depths of love and ambition, entwined in the engrossing story of *VINES*.

On a paper flag attached to the inside Bianca had pencilled: "If you have suggestions, let me know and I'll pass them on as my own."

I called her at home. "'Breathing with human emotion . . . '" I began.

"Yes, I know. It's just on the verge. But effective, don't you think? I wrote it myself, in fact—this is a third or fourth rewrite. You wouldn't believe what they sent me at first."

"It's terrific," I breathed.

"I thought you'd like it. But 'plumbs' bothers me. Any suggestions?"

I said I'd think about it. Next day I offered "plunges," but it turned out the jacket was already too far along and the cost of the additional letter at this point (it would involve resetting an entire line) made it out of the question.

Two weeks later Bianca sent me the promo material, intended mainly for booksellers. It included a foldout of the beautiful blonde in living color with the motto, *VINES—Let It Intoxicate You*, emblazoned above her receiving lips. Accompanying materials announced the advertising campaign in print ads and radio, advance reading copies and the dump. No mention was made, however, of a major gimmick originally planned by Marketing to launch the book in champagne.

Harrier had been trying to persuade an "under-recognized" California vineyard to produce miniatures of champagne (labeled "Fleur"), which would be given away free with copies sold in liquor stores. The plan had fallen through, however, as had the attempt to wrest a suitable quote from Irving J—, an author of Bianca's whose best-sellers were usually set in Paris. ("My dear," he had written in a personal note to her, "this is positively the worst—that is, least historically correct—book I've ever read on the war years in France. I advise you not to publish it, but if you

must, please do something about the most glaring inaccuracies."
He'd appended a list of them, for which Bianca and I were grateful, and the small changes were made at the last minute.)

Originally scheduled for a pub date in January during the lull after Christmas sales, the book had been moved up to a far riskier time, late spring, when it would have to compete with other novels slated for summer reading, endemic best sellers among them. We would wait, the Frog said, until after publication for our lunch at Lutèce. I was willing; the money I'd received so far had been disappearing in little scraps of paper, checks to cover the cost of existence for Becky and me.

The last installment of the advance was due on publication; after that we'd be receiving direct royalties as soon as the advance was made up. This would happen after about 250,000 copies were sold—or sooner, if any subsidiary rights came in: film or TV, first serial, or foreign.

The Frog was working on the outline for *Hearts,* vacillating in his decision to offer it before or after the publication of *Vines.* It was a gamble either way, he explained. We'd be asking three hundred; before publication, Harrier might offer two hundred, maybe even less. If *Vines* turned out to be a big money-maker, we'd lose; on the other hand . . .

I didn't know how to advise him. In March, the British rights to *Vines* were sold to Osprey, an affiliate of Harrier, for £40,000, or roughly $60,000. Since we were to receive eighty percent of foreign rights, this meant that nearly half the advance was already made up. He decided to wait.

April first, Bianca called to tell me that Dalton would be featuring *Vines* as its window display, and that Waldenbooks was doing the same. I thought she was too old for April Fool. A week later she called and asked if I was sitting down. I asked her who had died. "Two Sundays from now, *Vines* will be on *The New York Times* best-seller list," she said.

"'And I am the Queen of Roumania.'" Since pub date was still a month away, I knew she was continuing her irritable joking.

"Call them up yourself," she suggested, and gave me a phone number. It was a recorded message from the *Times,* announcing the best-seller list for Sunday, April 27. *Vines* by Jacqueline Knightsbridge was #11.

We stayed on the list for eight weeks, moving up as high as #6 before starting the descent. Winnie Silver sent me a bouquet of flowers large enough to cover the head and shoulders of the Derby winner. "Brilliant job, Jacqueline," she wrote on the card. Harrier was ecstatic, she said. Bianca was jubilant. I was incredulous. The Frog decided it was time to submit the new outline.

Collaborators

The fish terrine was moist inside the baked brioche. The wine gleamed pale gold above the slender stems. The Frog was turning purple, mouth agape.

When we finally had our lunch at Lutèce it was terrible. The conversation, not the food. I'd brought up the subject on the advice of a lawyer friend who'd said that, while he doubted Gernreich would agree to giving me a share in the Knightsbridge name, there could be no harm in asking.

That was possibly a fatal dose of understatement, I thought, watching his face deepen to a fine shade of cabernet. He sputtered, gagged, stopped eating his food. I felt sorry for him then, and afraid he might be having an apoplectic fit. Only a small share, I said, just a tiny part of Knightsbridge to call my own.

I might as well have been asking for a thin slice of kidney from one of his children. He remained speechless, waving his arms, opening and closing his mouth without emitting a sound. His eyes bulged as if electrified, their color draining from mud to silt. Waiters ran up to our table asking if they should bring water or call a doctor. He shooed them away with a brush of his hand and they scattered like grateful flies. I thought of Rumpelstiltskin—all that fuss about a name.

After several minutes, he recovered his voice. "Suppose you die?" he croaked.

"Excuse me?"

"You die, your kid inherits."

I was unprepared. "Suppose you die," I echoed. "Your kids inherit."

"Damn right. The kids and Dorianne. They get the rights to Knightsbridge." His wife Dorianne was a former gym-teacher who now worked on Wall Street, doing something with precious metals. The kids were young, first grade and fourth. Unless I'd seriously underestimated them, none of the three was capable of writing or even outlining a novel.

"So what?" he countered. "They can hire whoever they want. You think *you* had anything to do with Knightsbridge's success? I did it all. All. I could've written it myself too, except I knew it would be good for the book to have a woman on it." His palms were flat on the table, elbows hinged as if about to leap. "I was planning every step of the way, calculating all the time. Everything I did was to make her a winner. And that's what she is. Because of me. I made her and she's mine, one hundred percent. I don't need you and I never did. I could get anyone."

I was shaking my head, terrified. "No," I whispered. "I *wrote* it."

He relented, lowering his elbows as the duck was placed before him, its flesh rosy with blood, a red paler than burgundy, deeper than blush. "You're good for her," the Frog acknowledged. "You give her a certain class. I know that. I'm not about to spill the applecart. We make a great team." He was almost smiling, his color returning to normal. "You're good for her," he repeated, "and that means you're good for me. And I'm good for you. I'm making you rich. I'm teaching you things you'll be able to use even if you go back to writing under your own name again. You're worth something now."

I thought that was probably true, though I couldn't bring myself to thank him. "Way I figure it," he went on, switching to business, my ingratitude unnoticed, "Harrier's already owing us on *Vines*. We've made up the advance and we're due for royalties. Puts us in a great position for *Hearts*. I told Malady we're not taking less than three, and we want a hundred thou up front on signing."

He turned his attention to the duck, spearing the morsels and popping them into his mouth, his cheeks puffing out like a malevolent cherub's as he gulped them down, not bothering to chew. "But you know publishers, the way they try to hang on to their money. Leeches. It might take weeks, who knows, maybe even a month or two, before we finagle them into drawing up the contract the way we want it. Don't let that hold you back though." He polished off the bird and pushed the plate away, vegetables untouched. "You should be getting started right away. Here, I brought you my file of clippings"—he took it out from his briefcase, placed it on the table. "It's got surgery, of course, and also some good background material on the Italian fascists . . ." (Nazis or their allies were an essential part of the Knightsbridgean formula, their instantly recognizable evil drawing in the reader while providing her with Facts about the Second World War.) "You can begin work immediately. Don't wait till we sign. I've set up an appointment for us with the top heart man at Sinai a week from Wednesday."

He was keeping the pace breathless. No time to wonder, or to think. I put the file on the seat beside me. Also, he said, he'd found a woman heart surgeon at Presbyterian— "a redhead, about thirty-five. You'll want to talk to her on your own. Woman-to-woman, you might get more out of her." He handed me her card. "Call her this afternoon and arrange a meeting. Tempus fugit. We want *Hearts* out in time for Christmas, and that means handing it in to them by June latest. After that we'll be going for hardback with the third, and we're asking a million."

The waiter removed our plates and brought on the mocha soufflé we'd ordered at the beginning of the meal. It looked superb, but I'd had enough by then and left my share uneaten.

✍ ✍ ✍

We signed with Harrier for a $300,000 advance just after Labor

Day, though I was already at work on the book. Bianca edited each section as I wrote it, and the novel was completed six weeks before deadline.

The plot of *Hearts* followed the basic construction of *Vines*. Our heroine Val (from Valentina) was also born abroad, was orphaned of her mother at an early age, encountered sex for the first time in the arms of a woman, came to America as a child and struggled her way to the top of her profession. Like Fleur, she is challenged by a female rival, and like Fleur she resists love (but not sex) as she makes her lonely way in pursuit of her goal.

Both novels open on a moment of crisis in the present ("Which of you bastards took the President's organ?"—*Hearts*), and then move back in time, first to the simple past of her childhood and then further back, the past compounded in the youth of her parents, providing a rich—though not necessarily accurate—historical background (*Vines* has the war in France; *Hearts* includes the spectacle of Mussolini and Clara Pettachi hanging by their necks in the square of Milan) and then progressing forward, to link up with the moment of the novel's beginning. From there it moves quickly to climax and resolution. Fleur must wait till she's nearly forty to marry the man she loves, but Val marries comparatively young, during her internship, to become the wife of her mentor, Chris Russell, a world-famous heart surgeon (his name derived from Christiaan Bernard, via the philosopher), though later the marriage ends in divorce. According to the outline, Val then falls in love with a man closer to her age, Don Trounce, a financial superstar whose name is stamped on airplanes and on hotels designed to look like *palazzos* or mosques. He sets her up in her own clinic and introduces her to the richest and most powerful people in the world, some of whom will become her patients. Eventually she will perform the crucial heart transplant that saves the life of the American President.

In the writing of *Hearts,* and with Bianca's blessing, I made some changes. Before Val can marry him, Don is killed in a tragic plane crash (a plane crash can never be other than tragic; if I wrote: "Don Trounce was killed in a comic plane crash," I'd lose my reader's sympathy), and after a respectable period of mourning, Val returns to Chris, who has, of course, never stopped loving her. They remarry.

Second time round is better than the first. Val is older now, established, at the height of her career. She has saved the President's life, appeared on the cover of *People*, been interviewed by Barbara Walters and Ted Koppel and been chosen Woman of the Year by *Time*. She and Chris set up a joint practice. Working together, living together, hand in hand and heart to heart, Val and Chris become the Valentine couple of America.

The Frog didn't like it. Not exciting enough, he said: marrying the same person again was like seeing the same movie twice. Elizabeth Taylor had done it, I reminded him, and besides, some movies are better the second time. "You'll see," he warned, "This marriage is going to cost us. It puts a damper on *Hearts*."

Hearts went into production right after Memorial Day. We were due for another large check, and *Vines* was still selling. Eighteen foreign-language editions had been contracted for, and it was an unprecedented best-seller in England, with 200,000 copies sold in a week. I had never made so much money in my life. I needed an accountant, a tax lawyer, a financial advisor. I bought two sportcars, white and silver, for Becky and myself; to show his appreciation, the salesman gave me a bottle of champagne.

"All that will change," the Frog predicted. He was resenting ever more fiercely the closeness that had developed between Bianca and me; he felt we were in cahoots against him, undermining what he knew to be the formula for success. He had the pulse of

America's readers, he said. My tampering would kill the book. "You should've followed the outline."

✍ ✍ ✍

On November 15, *Hearts* hit the Big List as #5.

VI

THE FROG AND I

Vines was reprinted when *Hearts* came out; each of the novels sold over a million copies. The latest Knightsbridge will be published in the Fall of this year, but I'm no longer the author. I don't know who is. The Frog let me go after we'd signed a new contract. He'd meant to engage a scribe, not an equal, and when I'd asked for a share in our joint creation, he'd begun laying his plans. I didn't realize it then, though in hindsight it seems obvious. He saw himself as the sole creator of Knightsbridge, and was unwilling to share her name or even—as it later turned out—her profits with someone he regarded as merely a surrogate, hired to bring his conception to issue.

Malady tells me the Frog recently bought a town house on the Upper East Side, worth close to $4,000,000. She's not his agent anymore either; he got rid of her a few months after he'd gotten rid of me, which was shortly after we'd left Harrier and signed the $800,000 contract with Venom. (He'd insisted on leaving Harrier when they wouldn't offer anything above 750, and though he'd already decided to conceive future novels with a different writer, he'd kept me around for the signing with Venom, who thought they were getting the Knightsbridge of *Hearts* and *Vines*.) But Malady tells me that before he let her go, the Frog said, "Kate was the best one I had." I'm proud of that.

Malady still calls from time to time. Two weeks ago she said, "Drop everything," and I let go gingerly, the cat sliding from my lap. She'd been talking to a publisher who wanted a book on the state of the world. Why didn't I go back to my historical novel and bring it up to the revolutionary events in Eastern Europe and the Soviet Union? I thought about it awhile, realized I couldn't do it. You can't go home again, as maybe Hank Aaron said when he retired from baseball.

Sometimes Malady calls just to let me know what's up. She phoned after her lunch with Rebecca, the first writer hired by the Frog to replace me. Rebecca had left him after two months, but was only now recovering, Malady reported. "She says she'd rather give head in a Waldbaum's parking lot than work for that man ever again."

After he'd let me go, he turned to Malady again to procure another writer. She urged him to reconsider, but he was adamant; he needed fresh blood, he told her, and if she wouldn't provide it, he'd find someone else who could. Malady is an agent to her bones; at first she'd tried sending him a stream of women writers who, unable to find publishers for what they wrote, were willing to sell their souls to see their words in print. But with each new appli-

cant, Gernreich offered a lower percentage, haggling down the
retainer like Goneril or Regan: why twenty-five when twenty
would do? why so much? why twenty and not fifteen? why not ten?
Ten percent was more than generous. He argued that since he was
the one who'd made Knightsbridge into what she was, most of the
profit should by rights be his. As the pimp said to the whore.

"The best revenge is writing well," V says. She's back to her old
selves again. "Though maybe it's just writing."

After we broke up, I tried to get my revenge by doing a blockbuster on my own. It didn't work, of course, even though I disguised my name. There's more to writing such a book than simply
letting go of ego. You have to be able to plot furiously. That was
the Frog's genius. He was born to plot, and I was hopeless at it.

The money went. After the matching hers and hers sportscars, I
bought a few clothes of the kind that make you wish you had a life
to go with them. After that it was all taxes. The experts sheltered
me by locking half my earnings into a benefit plan to come due at
immortality or death, whichever came first, and with the rest I supported the federal government and New York State.

For a while, Mike and I tried collaborating on a novel about
elephants, but Mike was as bad at plotting as I was. Both of us had
a feel for characters, but we couldn't control them enough to fit
them into a scheme of events. You need a gift for management or
manipulation—not a way with people so much as around them.

Joseph Heller once told me he couldn't do plots either, and
that neither could Shakespeare. Maybe that's true, but both of
them knew how to pick one up someplace. Minor writers imitate;
major writers steal.

It was the inability to plot that toppled me from Knightsbridge
in the middle of round three, the novel about film-making

that starts out in Budapest during the uprising (Communists standing in for the Nazis). The outline ended when Magda was fifteen, though the story was to take our heroine to traditional Knightsbridgean climax at forty. Since I was bound to change his outline anyway, the Frog argued, it was a waste of time for him to write any more of it. He provided background, which I could have done myself, since Budapest was part of the Austro-Hungarian Empire my parents had been born into; also, I'd been there in the seventies to research my historical novel, had driven through the tunnel linking Buda to Pest and had gotten stuck in it with a Magyar poet who told me, "Tunnels are cunt." I had plenty of background, but no plot, and the Frog grew impatient. "If you don't think you can do it, I'll get someone else," he'd say in his kindest moments. The unkind ones were becoming more frequent and less coherent, his voice erupting on the phone with threats and accusations. It was obvious by now that he wanted me out, and I finally turned to a lawyer.

("Up to forty, it's sex," said Iris Owens, who wrote *After Claude;* "after that, it's all litigation." She was paraphrasing Gore Vidal, though I didn't know it.)

My lawyer was an old flame from pre-Arthurian days, a stunning piece of work who stood a fair and hefty six foot three, his nose set at a Brando-like angle through years of playing rugby. The touch of pugilism, added to otherwise Wasp-perfect features, made him a walking proposition. But, except for the thrill of coming into Malady's office with him at my side, like two Vikings bearing down on the small Frog and his smaller advocate, there was little he could do for me—no more than Faust's lawyer could have done for his client after the contract expired and the girl was plucked back. I had to sign a waiver of claims, now and in the future, giving up all rights to Knightsbridge, and to any part of her.

From start to finish, I had spent more than four years with the

Frog. When our contract ended, I gave up the part of myself that had belonged to him.

"The secret of happiness is a congenial monotony," wrote V. S. Pritchett, and I was impressed by the truth of that until I married. Then I wanted excitement, drama, a stage underfoot, and my audience in Arthur. When he fled the scene, the play lost meaning.

What do I know? If truth were essential to the writing of stories, there would be fewer writers than elephants left on the earth. Truth is as shifting as character; our friends are remarkable for only as long as they remain devoted to us.

I write in digressions. Montaigne viewed the universe through the filter of himself. Fiction uses many filters, the characters I create in my own image, who then return the courtesy by inventing me. But when Montaigne wrote about his closest friend in his *Apology for Raymond Sebond*, he said he loved the man, "because I am I and he is he."

Arthur is who he is. He's back, now that I'm no longer Knightsbridge. I call him Art. We're congenial and no more monotonous than breakfast. All happy families . . . The characters are returning.

Becky is engaged to a man named Pritchard who's ten years older than she is, a good old boy from Gator Swamps in one of the overheated states who Becky says can "write like an angel and make love like the devil." He's widely unpublished and drinks double martinis until he's cross-eyed. Becky wants to be a writer too, though she's studying biology in graduate school just in case she needs something more solid than words to fall back on. I think they'll be happy together; though Pritch is basically a misogynist (his term for all women is "mothers"), he treats Becky fairly, just like a man.

Mike attends elephant conferences where he meets zoo keepers, circus addicts and other interesting people to add to his collection. And V's play about the health club came out as a film last year, an instant classic among the cognoscenti. It opens on a suburban scene: Mother packing up her gym bag while her little boy asks riddles, trying to make her stay at home. *Where does the monster go when he loses a hand?* She smiles vaguely, zips it shut. *To the second-hand store.* She blows him a kiss, heads for the door. *Where should you go if you don't want to die?* She hesitates, then continues out to car as camera pans to titles; the name of the health club; voice-over: *The Living Room.*

Endings are difficult. If they're planned in advance, you rig the story to fit the outcome and it won't ring true; if you let them come naturally, they'll be too abrupt, or they linger infuriatingly, like guests who don't know how to say goodnight. I know of only two perfect endings, Dostoyevsky's "Ah what a way for it all to end!—what a glorious way to finish!" and Camus' "It is too late now. It will always be too late—happily," and at least one of these could be a beginning.

In my end is my beginning; in the beginning, the word. God to dog and deus to sued.

Gernreich is getting richer. His new agent is Ivan Bangkok, of Bangkok and Cockburn, the superagency that handles nothing under seven figures. Malady says they're asking $1.7 million for the next two-book Knightsbridge contract, but that Venom is waiting to see how the new book does before committing.

There's an ad for the upcoming Knightsbridge in the current issue of *PW* : "*Family Jewels* is an arousing saga of greed, passion and ambition . . . Irving J— calls it 'A perfect gem' . . . Book-of-the-Month Club Alternate Selection. By the best-selling author of *Vines* and *Hearts . . .*" etc.

What hurts most is not the money. It's remembering the sense of being alive, carried along by his will. "Being so caught up . . ." Leda and the Swan, me and the Frog. "So mastered . . ."— writing like a fiend.

Sometimes I still dream about the Frog. Last night I dreamed he came to visit me in the far-off mountains where I lived. I was very happy to see him. His skin was the color of money and when he touched me I was aroused. He had a new book for me to write, he said. We were sitting in the kitchen and the pages of my manuscript flew up and covered the table. I didn't want him to see that I'd been writing about him and tried to hide the pages with my body. But he could see through me. His eyes were glittering like emeralds, and I understood that he'd come to help me write it.

"*The Frog and I*—not a bad title," V says. She's working on a short novel in first person. "I think I'll use it."

"You can't . . . "

"Revenge takes many forms." She smiles. "Did I tell you? I've decided to name the narrator Kate."

"That's *my* book . . . " I begin, but already she's changing shape and voice.

Kathrin Perutz has nine earlier novels and two nonfiction works to her name, and her short pieces have appeared in a wide range of publications as diverse as *American Scholar, Harper's, Cosmopolitan, Vogue,* and the *New York Times.* She sits on the PEN Executive Board and has been a fellow at both the MacDowell and Yaddo colonies and the Virginia Center for the Creative Arts. She lives in Great Neck, New York.